WORLD ECONOMIC AND FINANCIAL SURVEYS

Trade Liberalization in IMF-Supported Programs

Prepared by a Staff Team led by Robert Sharer

with
Piritta Sorsa
Nur Calika
Paul Ross
Clinton Shiells
Thomas Dorsey

INTERNATIONAL MONETARY FUND
Washington, DC
February 1998

Cataloging-in-Publication Data
Trade liberalization in IMF-supported programs /
prepared by a staff team led by Rober Sharer with Piritta Sorsa . . . [et al.]. — Washington, DC : International Monetary Fund
p. cm. — (World economic and financial surveys, ISSN 0258-7440)

Includes bibliographical references.
ISBN1-55775-707-0

1. Commercial policy. 2. Free trade. 3. International Monetary Fund. I. Sharer, Rober L. II. Sorsa, Piritta, 1955-III Series. HF1411.T73 1998

Price: US$25.00
(US$20.00 to full-time faculty members and
students at universities and colleges)

Please send orders to:
International Monetary Fund, Publication Services
700 19th Street, N.W., Washington, D.C. 20431, U.S.A.
Tel.: (202) 623-7430 Telefax: (202) 623-7201
E-mail: publications@imf.org
Internet: http://www.imf.org

recycled paper

Contents

Figures
Section

The following symbols have been used throughout this volume:

. . . to indicate that data are not available;

— to indicate that the figure is zero or less than half the final digit shown, or that the item does not exist;

– between years or months (for example, 1995–96 or January–June) to indicate the years or months covered, including the beginning and ending years or months;

/ between years (for example, 1995/96) to indicate a fiscal or financial year.

"Billion" means a thousand million; "trillion" means a thousand billion.

"Basis points" refer to hundredths of 1 percentage point (for example, 25 basis points are equivalent to ¼ of 1 percentage point).

"n.a." means not applicable.

Minor discrepancies between constituent figures and totals are due to rounding.

As used in this volume the term "country" does not in all cases refer to a territorial entity that is a state as understood by international law and practice. As used here, the term also covers some territorial entities that are not states but for which statistical data are maintained on a separate and independent basis.

Preface

This study assesses trade liberalization in programs supported by the International Monetary Fund based on a review of multiyear arrangements in the 1990s and on six detailed case studies. The review compares the initial degree of restrictiveness of each country's trade regime, each program's trade liberalization objectives, and the degree of trade restrictiveness at the end of the program. It then discusses the main economic factors affecting trade policy targets, including in particular the impact of fiscal considerations. The case studies extend this effort to program design and negotiation, and the key factors relevant to implementation.

The study was prepared in the Trade Policy Division of the Policy Development and Review Department (PDR) of the Fund. The principal authors of the study are Robert Sharer, Division Chief; Piritta Sorsa, Deputy Division Chief; Nur Calika, Paul Ross, and Clinton Shiells, Senior Economists; and Thomas Dorsey, Economist. Valuable inputs were provided for the study by Kamau Thugge, Senior Economist; Inutu Lukonga, Bradley McDonald, Leslie Teo, Nicholas Tsaveas, and Ricardo Velloso, all Economists; and Dustin Smith, Research Assistant.

The authors are indebted to Jack Boorman, Director, and Oleh Havrylyshyn, at the time Assistant Director (PDR), for their guidance in preparation of the study. Acknowledgment is due to numerous colleagues in the Fund for their willingness to exchange views and provide information, and to Professor Anne Krueger for helpful comments. The authors are grateful to Juanita Roushdy of the External Affairs Department for editing the manuscript and coordinating production of the publication and to Mary Joanne Marquez and Shirley Davies for expert word-processing assistance. The authors alone are responsible for the study; any opinions expressed are theirs and do not necessarily reflect the views of the Fund.

List of Abbreviations

CBI	Cross-Border Initiative
CEFTA	Central European Free Trade Agreement
CMEA	Council for Mutual Economic Assistance
COMESA	Common Market for Eastern and Southern Africa
EFF	Extended Fund Facility
ERS	Export retention scheme
ESAF	Enhanced Structural Adjustment Facility
EU	European Union
FTA	Free trade area
GATT	General Agreement on Tariffs and Trade
GDP	Gross domestic product
IMF	International Monetary Fund
ISAC	Industrial sector adjustment credit
MFN	Most favored nation
NTB	Nontariff barrier
OGIL	Open general import license
QR	Quantitative restriction
RAP	Rights Accumulation Program
RTA	Regional trading arrangement
SAF	Structural Adjustment Facility
SAL	Structural Adjustment Loan
UNCTAD	United Nations Conference on Trade and Development
UR	Uruguay Round
VAT	Value-added tax
WTO	World Trade Organization

I

Introduction

Trade reform is an important aspect of the Fund's purposes and objectives. Article I of its Articles of Agreement explicitly refers to the importance of trade for economic prosperity and growth.[1] The Fund's role in the area of trade policy is complementary to that of other international institutions, in particular, the World Bank and the World Trade Organization (WTO) (Box 1).[2]

[1]Article I (ii) states that the Fund is "To facilitate the expansion and balanced growth of international trade, and to contribute thereby to the promotion and maintenance of high levels of employment and real income and to the development of the productive resources of all members as primary objectives of economic policy."

[2]The Fund and the WTO have concluded a Cooperation Agreement that came into effect on December 9, 1996.

This study assesses trade liberalization in Fund-supported programs based on a review of multiyear arrangements in the 1990s and on six detailed case studies. It has a review section which compares the initial degree of restrictiveness of each country's trade regime, each program's trade liberalization objectives, and the degree of trade restrictiveness at the end of the program. The study then discusses the main economic factors affecting trade policy targets, including in particular the impact of fiscal considerations. The case studies extend this effort to program design and negotiation, and the key factors relevant to implementation.

This study finds that there was a clear need for trade liberalization in the programs reviewed, since the ma-

Box 1. The Roles of the Fund, the WTO, and the World Bank in Trade Policy

The WTO,[1] successor to the General Agreement on Tariffs and Trade (GATT), is a rules-based institution that provides a common institutional framework for the conduct of trade relations among its members. Through the "binding" of negotiated tariff concessions and the application of agreed rules, it improves security and predictability of market access in world trade. The WTO commitments and rules are limitations on the maximum amount of protection, not optimal levels from the point of view of individual countries' economic efficiency. They also provide for numerous exceptions, allow long and variable transition periods, and afford some categories of members special treatment. Moreover, they do not address fully a number of important aspects of trade policy with significant structural and macroeconomic implications that include export taxes, state trading monopolies, tariff dispersion, and import tariff exemptions. Because the WTO serves primarily as a forum for discussions among members, it is largely through periodic multilateral trade negotiations, the dispute settlement mechanism, and the accession process that trade policies of individual members are influenced; the WTO also conducts periodic trade policy reviews with members. Procedures have been set up to ensure that Fund advice in member countries' trade reforms is consistent with their WTO obligations. Fund policy advice is oriented to improve economic efficiency and thus may go beyond WTO commitments. As a result, the IMF, through surveillance and, more specifically, within its program support, may seek broader-based and faster trade reform than provided for by WTO agreements. However, in contrast to WTO commitments, such reform would not be "bound" and may, therefore, be subject to reversals should circumstances change.

The Fund and the World Bank collaborate closely on trade policy issues in the context of adjustment programs. The Bank often takes the lead when there are complex and detailed tariff reforms or industry- and sector-specific trade policies in which the Bank has recognized expertise. Some World Bank adjustment operations have focused exclusively on trade reform. On the other hand, the Fund has focused on encouraging market-oriented policies to improve the efficiency of resource allocation and promote growth through the expansion of trade, within an appropriate macroeconomic framework, with policies to promote the liberalization of the trade system, including the removal of quantitative restrictions and other nontariff barriers and moving toward reasonably uniform low tariffs. The Fund sometimes takes the lead, particularly whenever the Bank's operations do not address trade policy, or where Fund technical assistance is provided on the reform and administration of tariffs and trade taxes. Differences in timing between the Bank and the Fund in stabilization and structural reform programs sometimes lead to greater Fund involvement in trade reform.

[1]Of the 181 Fund members, 126 are members of the WTO and 29 are in accession discussions.

jority of countries started out with restrictive trade systems. Two-thirds of programs targeted a quantifiable reduction in restrictiveness, as measured by the index used in the study. One-third of programs, however, did not target any quantifiable change, including programs for countries starting with restrictive trade regimes. Programs generally achieved their targeted trade reform objectives, and there was a marked movement in the aggregate trade policy stance of the countries reviewed toward less restrictive regimes. The strength of conditionality was related to the importance of the measure for the program, and it appears to have facilitated implementation. More liberalization, however, should probably have been targeted in a significant number of programs, particularly in countries with initially restrictive regimes.

The appropriate level of ambitiousness is discussed in relation to a country's initial trade regime and the experience of a group of "good practice" countries that moved to open trade regimes over seven to ten years. While the programs in restrictive countries that did not target reform were clearly unambitious, extensive trade reform was achieved in a substantial number of programs. In the case study countries, virtually all trade liberalization during the 1990s occurred in the context of Fund programs. Although some statement regarding medium-term trade liberalization objectives was mentioned at the outset in two-thirds of the arrangements, they were generally insufficiently comprehensive or detailed to permit effective monitoring.

Fiscal policy concerns were often cited as an important factor limiting the extent of trade reform targeted. However, a review of fiscal indicators and evidence that more fiscally neutral trade policies may have been available do not always support such caution. At the same time, the case studies indicate that the design of successful programs was done in a way to counter fiscal or other concerns raised at the outset. This included focusing initially on the removal of nontariff barriers (NTBs), with potentially revenue-reducing tariff reform left to a later stage and by introducing broader-based taxes and targeting a reduction in exemptions. This suggests that some programs could perhaps have targeted more far-reaching trade reform.

A significant factor for successful liberalization in the countries studied was the authorities' commitment to expeditious implementation of trade reform and liberal market-oriented policies, as well as ownership of the program. This manifested itself in trade reform being viewed as a key medium-term objective with preannounced targets, which was found to be important in program implementation. World Bank involvement was frequently cited as having influenced trade reform and the results of Fund-Bank collaboration in this area seem to have been effective.

II

Analytical Framework and Elements of Trade Reform

A liberal trade regime is an important factor in encouraging economic growth and efficient resource allocation. The case for open trade policies and consequent resource allocation improvements and enhanced medium-term growth prospects are well known and supported by a large body of theoretical and empirical work (Box 2).

The success of trade reform depends on complementary macroeconomic policies. In particular, there are strong and mutually supporting links between trade reform, an appropriate level for the real exchange rate, and a liberal exchange system, because exchange and trade restrictions often act as substitutes and the benefits of liberalizing one may not be fully realized without liberalizing the other. In one direction, an open trade regime is needed so that international price signals promote efficient resource allocation for a country with an appropriate real exchange rate and a liberal exchange regime. In the other direction, an appropriate exchange rate and a liberal exchange regime are needed so that the tradables sector can exploit its comparative advantage and maintain the momentum of trade liberalization efforts and macroeconomic stabilization. In particular, if the exchange rate is overvalued, then a real depreciation may be an important complement to trade liberalization. If the exchange rate is maintained at an artificially high level or there are equivalent exchange sys-

Box 2. Trade and Growth

The economic rationale for trade policy reform is based on the improved efficiency of resource allocation and enhanced growth prospects. An open trade regime expands trade and investment options and allows countries to specialize in and export those products in which they have a comparative advantage. Trade barriers to imports result in higher prices for imported commodities and cause inefficiency as consumers shift to higher cost domestic substitutes or forgo use or consumption of products they would otherwise prefer. Import barriers also give rise to an anti-export bias through higher costs to exporters, the impact on the exchange rate which tends to be more appreciated, and because import-competing industries tend to bid workers and capital away from would-be exporters or other potentially more efficient economic activities.

The efficiency benefits of an open trade policy also apply to economic growth. In common with other economic distortions, trade policy distortions shift an economy to a less efficient mix of investment, production, and consumption. They create incentives to produce and invest in goods for which the economy's rate of return is below the rate of return for the individual enterprise. These distortions depress economic growth prospects and their removal therefore improves growth prospects. Indeed, it is even possible in a distorted trade regime that new investment or increases in other factor supplies can reduce national income—so-called immiserizing growth.[1]

The empirical literature on trade and growth confirms and underscores the theoretical case for open trade policies; namely, that countries with open trade policies grow faster than countries that are more inward oriented.[2] These findings have been emphasized by a number of recent studies, including work using very extensive time series data (Summers and Heston, 1991), and also by new developments in the theory of economic growth such as endogenous growth theory that has highlighted dynamic gains from trade liberalization. Moreover these findings provide further credibility and confirmation that trade openness is consistently associated with higher rates of economic growth, as measured by trade-to-GDP ratios (Barro and Sala-i-Martin, 1995); trade protectionism (Sachs and Warner, 1995); more indirect techniques designed to control for reverse causality and other statistical anomalies (Frankel, Romer, and Cyrus, 1996); and when growth is measured by per capita GDP growth or by productivity measures (Coe and Helpman, 1993).

[1]See Bhagwati and Srinivasan (1983) for a summary and further elaboration in the context of other trade distortions and Brecher and Diaz-Alejandro (1977) for the case of mmiserizing foreign investment inflows in the context of trade policy distortions.

[2]The general results and summaries of the literature have been included in World Bank (1987 and 1991); the IMF (1993); World Bank (1993); and Kirmani and others (1994b).

Box 3. Political Economy and Trade Reform

In the extensive economic literature on the political economy of trade policy, a seminal article by Anne Krueger (1974) presents estimates showing the "windfall" transfers of resources ("rents") resulting from the effects of successful lobbying and similar legal or illegal activities that influence trade policy (5 percent and 15 percent of GDP in examples from India and Turkey, respectively). She presents a model in which "rent seeking" (comprising both legal activities such as lobbying and illegal activities such as bribery) lowers the efficiency of the economy, particularly when quotas are used instead of tariffs. The resources used in rent seeking to encourage governments to adopt inefficient trade policies and to allocate valuable licenses to the seekers are wasted for the economy because they are not available for productive uses. Tariffs are preferable to an equivalently restrictive quota because the rents associated with the windfall gain to holders of quota rights will encourage more rent seeking than a tariff, where the tariffs on imports are captured by the government in the form of tariff revenue.

In the years since, a large and complex literature has evolved on the political economy of economic policy formation that heavily focuses on trade policies. Important extensions to the literature have been made by Bhagwati (1982), and a large part of the literature has been summarized at book length with many original contributions by Magee, Brock, and Young (1989). Summaries of still more recent contributions as well as original material can be found in Krueger (1993), Williamson (1994), Rodrik (1995), and Leidy (1995). The *1997 World Development Report* (World Bank, 1997) provides an extensive applied discussion of the interactions between economic policy (including trade policy) and political economy considerations. Some general, although diverse, lessons do emerge from this literature. First, political intervention by economic interest groups cannot be relied upon to bring about efficient trade policies. As noted in the study, there is a tendency for the relatively concentrated and organized import-competing producers to be more successful in obtaining protection than for the relatively dispersed consumers in resisting it; empirical support for the influence of these factors and for the tendency of protection to be higher for products in which import-competing producers have declining profits and sales can be found in Baldwin (1985). Indeed, under some assumptions it can be relied upon to result in inefficient economic policies. Second, complex and nontransparent trade regimes are particularly vulnerable to both bad policies resulting from rent seeking and to the waste of resources used in rent seeking. Even though interest groups need to expend more effort to modify complex and nontransparent systems, the more narrowly focused rents and the difficulties in monitoring rents for society at large can raise the cost-benefit ratio to the rent seeker. This is part of the basis for the argument for a uniform tariff. Third, policies that generate private windfalls rather than government revenue (e.g., quotas or tariff exemptions rather than tariffs) are particularly conducive to the distortions induced by rent seeking. Finally, recent literature (see Krueger, 1993 and Rodrik, 1995) has emphasized the virtuous circle that can develop as vested interests in rents from trade policy distortions are reduced and vested interests in exporting are increased.

The tendency toward adverse policy outcomes and wasted resources from rent seeking suggests a role for an outside agency such as the Fund. For Fund-supported programs, the implications of the political economy literature described above on quotas versus tariffs and simple versus complex systems support moves toward simpler and more transparent tariff-based systems on the path to overall liberalization. Finally, the literature on turning vicious circles of rent seeking into virtuous circles of liberalization underlines the need for sustained efforts toward trade liberalization.

tem distortions, the political and economic support for open trade policies can be undermined.[3] There are also strong and mutually supporting links between trade reform and fiscal policy, which are discussed in Section III. In general, the beneficial effects of trade reform are best realized in an appropriate macroeconomic environment and in tandem with other structural reform policies to improve the efficiency of resource allocation.

Elements of Trade Liberalization

The main goal of trade reform should be to improve economic efficiency by creating a transparent and neutral system of incentives that eliminates anti-export bias, direct impediments to trade, and economic distortions caused by the trade regime. This would involve removing export barriers and quantitative restrictions (QRs) and other NTBs[4] on imports,

[3]Exchange rate policy and exchange reform are linked in important ways to trade policy but generally fall outside the scope of trade liberalization, narrowly defined, and hence are generally excluded from this study, except where such restrictions act as binding trade restrictions.

[4]Nontariff barriers are defined here as measures that restrict trade by either limiting quantities that may be traded or inserting administrative discretion in the export-import process that acts as a barrier to trade. Such NTBs include quantitative restrictions, quotas, bans, restrictive licensing requirements, restrictive foreign exchange practices, state trading monopolies, restrictive technical and phytosanitary standards, and restrictive customs procedures.

reducing tariff dispersion through introducing low and relatively uniform tariffs[5] administered in a transparent and evenhanded manner, and establishing neutral treatment of imports and domestic goods under domestic economic policies.[6] Trade reform is often sequenced so that initial action on import barriers focuses on QRs and other NTBs,[7] which tend to be the most distortionary trade restrictions. Measures to reform import tariffs include reductions in the maximum and higher tariffs and in the number of tariff bands; conversion of specific tariffs into ad valorem rates; consolidation of other import taxes or charges into a single rate; and reduction or elimination of tariff exemptions for individuals, organizations, or groups. Trade reform may also include other measures to ensure equal treatment of domestic and imported goods, and it implies an absence of controls on domestic trade, such as price or marketing controls.

Transparency, Governance, and Political Economy

Trade liberalization is intended, in the first instance, to improve resource allocation and economic welfare; it also has important beneficial effects on the transparency of the trade system and the quality of governance. Because of their highly disaggregated nature, trade policies are particularly suited to the redirection of resources by the government to narrow interest groups (Box 3). Transparency is an issue because those adversely affected by trade policy are often affected indirectly and may not be aware of the effect. Liberalization and simplification can reduce this adverse impact and improve the ability of those affected by the policy to detect and understand the impact of the remaining trade policy instruments. Even beyond legal but inefficient and nontransparent rent seeking, complex and discretionary trade policy regimes create opportunities for corruption (particularly in the case of discretionary licensing and tariff exemptions). Broad-based and comprehensive trade reforms, preferably preannounced, can contribute importantly to improved governance.

Usually, the most important impediments to trade reform are political economy factors.[8] In some cases, they may be a response to the economic adjustment costs and disruption that may be associated with significant policy changes that improve the efficiency of resource allocation. In trade reform, the most concentrated group of losers are usually readily identifiable producers facing the loss of existing sources of income, while beneficiaries are widely dispersed among consumers and potential exporters that may be difficult to identify. However, beyond adjustment costs, the often highly focused economic impact of trade policy makes it a particularly attractive target of rent-seeking behavior and lobbying, in many cases, by small well-organized groups, while the costs associated with restrictive trade policies are widely dispersed throughout the economy and are not transparent. These political economy factors, together with the government's commitment to liberal market-oriented reforms, "ownership" of the program, and garnering political support, are likely to be the most critical factors in effective trade reform.

[5]Uniform tariffs are preferable on political economy grounds since they reduce the incentive to lobby for a higher tariff rate. However, uniform nominal tariff rates need not imply uniform effective rates of protection if, for instance, domestic taxes are higher in some sectors; see Thomas, Nash, and others (1991).

[6]This includes equal tax treatment of domestic and foreign entities, equal tax treatment of imported and domestic goods and services, and equal technical and phytosanitary standards.

[7]Often import quantitative restrictions are replaced by tariffs.

[8]Political economy forces may be working in favor of trade liberalization, for example, to foster closer relationships with neighboring countries.

III

Review of Fund Arrangements and Assessment of Overall Results

To assess trade policy in Fund-supported programs,[9] a review was conducted of all multiyear arrangements initiated and terminated between January 1990 and June 1996.[10] The review examined trade reform targeted and implemented during the program period, and noted factors that influenced trade reform. This section first describes the methodology, then assesses the restrictiveness of countries' trade regimes at the start of the program, the targeted change in restrictiveness envisaged, and the overall restrictiveness at the end of the program. It continues with a discussion of program targets, monitoring, overall results, and ambitiousness, and factors that influenced trade reform in the programs and some implications for program design.

The review finds that (1) there was a clear need for trade liberalization in Fund-supported programs, since most countries started out with restrictive or highly restrictive systems; (2) the extent of movement toward liberal trade regimes targeted in Fund programs varied; about two-thirds of programs targeted a quantifiable reduction in restrictiveness measured by the index used in this study; (3) one-third of programs did not target a quantifiable change in trade restrictiveness, including those for countries starting with restrictive trade systems; (4) programs that targeted a reduction in restrictiveness generally succeeded in achieving their trade reform objectives, including through the appropriate use of binding monitoring (prior actions, performance criteria, benchmarks, and reviews); (5) medium-term trade reform targets although mentioned often were generally insufficiently specific and comprehensive; (6) in general, longer-term Fund involvement in countries during 1990–96 does not seem to have promoted greater trade liberalization in the programs reviewed; (7) the World Bank's involvement was frequently cited as having influenced trade reform, and the results of Fund-Bank collaboration seem to have been effective; and (8) fiscal concerns were an important factor limiting the extent of trade reform targeted, but no clear relationship was found between the strength of trade reform targets or achievements and the countries' fiscal objectives and circumstances.

Methodology

The following subsections describe the coverage of programs as well as the method used to measure the trade policy restrictiveness of the program countries.

Selection of Review Countries

The review covers multiyear Fund arrangements of at least two years' duration, since these are intended to target structural reform measures, including trade reform. Arrangements that came into effect after January 1, 1990 and that ended by June 30, 1996 were selected to facilitate evaluation of program outcomes. This resulted in the review covering 30 arrangements in support of 28 programs in 27 countries (Table 1).[11] While the number of programs is limited, the review covers a wide variety of countries and circumstances.

The review provides a snapshot of trade reform in each program and does not consider directly trade reform prior to, or following, the arrangements under review;[12] however, the issue of continued Fund involvement during the 1990s in the trade reform efforts of countries is discussed. While programs for three transition economies (Hungary, Mongolia, and Poland) were included, the selection criteria led to the exclusion of the Baltics, Russia, and other former Soviet Union countries. One reason for this was that during the early 1990s Fund support for these countries took the form of shorter-term programs supported by Stand-By Arrangements or the Systemic Transformation Facility. More important, these programs were applied in

[9]This assessment of trade policy does not imply any judgment of overall program content. Throughout this study, the terms "Fund-supported programs" and "Fund programs" are used interchangeably.

[10]The focus on multiyear arrangements introduces some bias in the sample group of arrangements toward Structural Adjustment Facility (SAF) and Enhanced Structural Adjustment Facility (ESAF) programs with low-income countries. These account for 19 of the 30 arrangements reviewed.

[11]There were two arrangements for Burkina Faso: a SAF in 1991 and an ESAF in 1993. The policy programs supported by these arrangements were distinct and separate. There were three arrangements for Zimbabwe but were in support of one policy program.

[12]Thus it does not cover significant trade reform efforts that may have occurred preceding or following the program under review, as was the case, for example, in Guyana, Jordan, Panama, and Peru.

Table 1. Arrangements Included in the Review of Fund-Supported Programs[1]
(Multiyear arrangements started after January 1, 1990 and completed by June 30, 1996)

	ESAF	EFF	SAF	Stand-By Arrangement
Africa				
Benin	1/25/93			
Burkina Faso	3/31/93		3/13/91	
Comoros			6/21/91	
Equatorial Guinea	2/3/93			
Ethiopia			10/28/92	
Lesotho	5/22/91			
Mali	8/28/92			
Mauritania	12/9/92			
Mozambique	6/1/90			
Sierra Leone[2]	4/3/92			
Tanzania	7/29/91			
Zambia[2]	7/17/92			
Zimbabwe	9/11/92	1/24/92		
		9/11/92		
Asia				
Bangladesh	8/10/90			
Mongolia	6/25/93			
Nepal	10/5/92			
Philippines				2/20/91
Sri Lanka	9/13/91			
Europe				
Hungary		2/20/91		
Poland		4/18/91		
Middle East				
Egypt				5/17/91
Jordan				2/26/92
Western Hemisphere				
Argentina		3/31/92		
Guyana	7/13/90			
Jamaica		12/11/92		
Panama				2/24/92
Peru		3/18/93		

Source: IMF.
[1]Stand-By Arrangement, Extended Fund Facility (EFF), Structural Adjustment Facility (SAF), Enhanced Structural Adjustment Facility (ESAF), and Rights Accumulation Program (RAP). Includes multiyear programs (at least two years long) that expired at the latest by the end of June 1996. The ESAF arrangements with Burundi and Rwanda, both of which began in 1991, are excluded.
[2]Rights Accumulation Program.

highly unusual circumstances. International trade had been administered in the context of the Council for Mutual Economic Assistance (CMEA), central planning was being dismantled, and the trade instruments used in market economies were not widely in place. In light of these exceptional circumstances the experiences of these programs are not replicable for other countries. Moreover, these experiences have been discussed in detail elsewhere. Nevertheless, several of these short-term programs achieved substantial structural change, including trade liberalization. The trade reforms of these countries are summarized in Box 4.

Quantification of the Overall Trade Policy Stance

Measurement of trade liberalization in the countries reviewed was based on an index of overall trade policy restrictiveness, which is discussed extensively in Appendix I.[13] The index consists of a 10-point scale that combines measurements of the restrictiveness of tariffs and NTBs. It measures the overall restrictiveness of a country's trade system relative to protection levels in all Fund members. The restrictiveness of the import tariff regime was based on the average unweighted statutory tariff rate, classified into five categories, from open to restrictive. The ranges of tariff rates used for classification were based on tariff rates of all Fund members; roughly equal numbers of Fund members fall in each category. Nontariff barriers were

[13]Appendix I discusses the classification of tariff and NTB regimes, how the 10-point scale combines tariff and NTB measures, and how other studies have quantified the overall restrictiveness of trade regimes in developing countries.

Box 4. Trade Reform in the Baltics, Russia, and Other Countries of the Former Soviet Union

The criteria used to select arrangements included in the review resulted in the exclusion of arrangements with the Baltics, Russia, and other former Soviet Union countries, as none of these countries had Fund arrangements of at least two years' duration that started after January 1, 1990 and ended by June 30, 1996. Nevertheless, trade liberalization was a key aspect of Fund programs in these countries and considerable liberalization was achieved. This box briefly reviews these trade liberalization achievements.[1]

In terms of initial conditions, the trade system had to be radically redesigned in all these countries. This was due to the role of central planning in trade, which was affected by the collapse of the CMEA and dismantling of barter trade agreements. Also, in many countries no trade system existed, because they were formerly part of a larger country. Trade reform and the accompanying move to a market-based exchange rate system were designed to provide price signals and a market-oriented incentive structure. This was aimed at restructuring domestic industry and export sectors to make the economies outward looking, globally integrated, and market based.

Fund programs, in collaboration with the World Bank, targeted the creation of simple, transparent, and tariff-based trade regimes. The Fund's trade policy advice had three main components. One was to remove quantitative restrictions (QRs). This was linked to the elimination of state trading and state orders, ensuring that QRs were not introduced, and where necessary replacing QRs on exports with temporary export taxes. The other two components involved eliminating expeditiously export taxes and adopting an import tariff structure that was low and relatively uniform. The legacy of central planning meant that much of the initial trade reform was focused on removing export QRs.

Generally, substantial progress in trade liberalization has been made. The magnitude of liberalization has varied across countries. Most progress has been made with removing quantity-based export restrictions that were inherited from central planning. This includes dismantling of state trading and rights of strategic exporters. The incidence of QRs on imports varies, but most countries use them sparingly. Many countries have also introduced low and uniform tariffs. In some cases, progress toward implementing a low and uniform import tariff structure has been influenced by the inability to mobilize fiscal revenue from other sources. In other cases, considerations relating to accession to the World Trade Organization or regional trading arrangements, or both, have affected the pace of trade liberalization.

[1]For a more detailed description, see Kirmani and others (1994a) and Leidy and Ibrahim (1996).

classified into three categories based on coverage and restrictiveness, including both import and export QRs, bans, and restrictive licensing, state trading monopolies, restrictive foreign exchange practices (where they acted as binding trade restrictions), and other NTBs.[14] A rating of 1 on the index represents the most open trade regime, and 10 the most restrictive. The index gives relatively more weight to NTBs since, as noted above, they generally result in larger economic distortions and less transparent policy regimes than high tariff rates.

Changes in tariff dispersion, maximum tariffs, exemptions, export taxes, and improvements in customs administration were not explicitly incorporated into the overall index due to the complexity of aggregating additional dimensions of trade policy and the difficulties of obtaining comparable cross-country data on these variables. In many cases, however, most of these additional measures of restrictiveness moved together with average tariff levels. Thus, by including average tariffs, the index implicitly captures, at least to some extent, these other measures of restrictiveness.

A variety of sensitivity analyses were undertaken to assess whether the results of the review would be significantly affected by changes in the tariff and NTB classifications. First, an alternative import tariff classification with wider tariff ranges was specified. This left virtually unchanged the extent of movement toward liberalization targeted and achieved. Next, NTB categories were redefined by omitting export restrictions as well as foreign exchange restrictions that acted as binding trade restraints; the results were essentially unchanged in each case. While in principle the index may miss significant trade liberalization at the restrictive end, examination of the data shows this rarely occurred in the programs reviewed and did not affect the results of the study.

Aggregation of different types of trade restrictions is not without challenges. Ideally, assessment of the overall restrictiveness of the trade regime should capture the distortions in relative prices and resource allocation due to the trade regime. In practice, construction of such measures requires very substantial amounts of information and analysis. As discussed in Appendix I, in comparison with the main previous studies of trade liberalization in developing countries, the index used here

[14]Other NTBs include safeguard actions, antidumping and countervailing duties, reference prices, quality controls, and indicative export prices.

Figure 1. Distribution of Overall Restrictiveness, Initial Conditions[1]

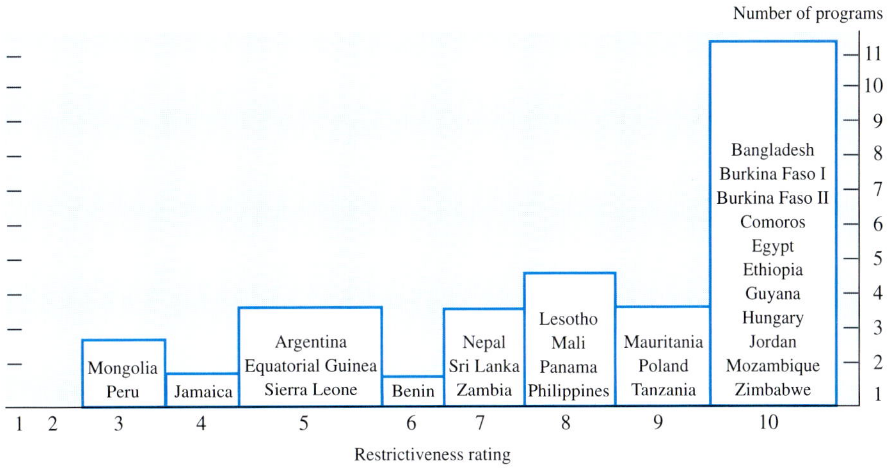

Source: IMF staff estimates.
[1]"Initial conditions" correspond to Fund arrangements that came into effect as indicated in Table 2.

has several advantages. Previous studies have (1) presented tariff and NTB measures separately without attempting to form an overall index of restrictiveness; or (2) developed very simple binary indicators of openness; or (3) conducted massive case studies to develop quantitative summary measures, such as effective rates of protection and effective exchange rates for exports and imports. This study adopts an intermediate approach that goes further than the first two categories toward providing comprehensive, objective measures of the overall stance of countries' trade regimes, while avoiding the large resource costs of the third method. While the results of the latter may be "state of the art" in their greater precision, they too are subject to important theoretical limitations.

Review of Multiyear Fund-Supported Programs, 1990–96

The overall openness of the trade systems prior to the beginning of programs covered by the review is summarized in Figure 1.[15] As can be seen, at the start of the programs, two-thirds of the countries reviewed were characterized by restrictive trade regimes, with classification of 8–10 on the index.[16] Indeed, almost 40 percent of the countries reviewed had highly restrictive regimes, classified at 10 on the index.[17] The preponderance of ratings in the restrictive category clearly highlights the need for trade liberalization.

Reflecting the profile of overall restrictiveness, import tariffs could also be classified as generally restrictive; tariff rates were widely dispersed for many of the programs reviewed. Exemptions also add to tariff dispersion; the existence of exemptions, which are not reflected in the tariff measures included in the index, was explicitly noted in the initial conditions in half of the 28 programs.

Regarding NTBs, again reflecting the profile of overall restrictiveness, many ratings were at or near the restrictive end of the scale. In addition to the many cases of quantitative restrictions on imports and exports (in the forms of quotas, bans, or restrictive licensing), state trading monopolies, usually covering commodities described as vital to the national interest, were mentioned in 17 programs.

Trade Reform Objectives

The extent of movement toward an open trade regime targeted in the Fund-supported programs re-

[15]It should be noted that analysis of the initial conditions of the trade system refers to the state of the trade policy regime before implementation of any prior actions under the program. Prior actions are included in the set of measures considered in assessing ambitiousness of program targets.

[16]For the analysis, countries with index classifications of 8–10 can be considered restrictive; classifications of 5–7, moderate; and classifications of 1–4, open.

[17]The finding that trade regimes were restrictive at the outset of programs is consistent with evidence in the IMF's 1997 ESAF review (Bredenkamp and others, 1998) that, starting from a situation of relatively restrictive regimes, countries using ESAF resources made only moderate progress in trade liberalization between 1985 and 1990; it should be noted that the coverage of countries differed in the two studies.

Table 2. Initial Overall Rating and Targeted Change in Restrictiveness Rating[1]

	Initial Overall Rating	Targeted Overall Change	Targeted NTB Change	Targeted Tariff Change	Targeted Overall Rating	Final Overall Rating
Mozambique (1990)	**10**	-4	-1	-2	6	6
Zimbabwe (1992)	**10**	-4	-1	-2	6	8
Burkina Faso II (1993)	**10**	-3	-1	0	7	7
Hungary (1991)	**10**	-3	-1	0	7	6
Bangladesh (1990)	**10**	-2	-1	0	8	8
Comoros (1991)	**10**	-2	-1	0	8	8
Egypt (1991)	**10**	-2	-1	0	8	8
Ethiopia (1992)	**10**	-2	-1	0	8	8
Guyana (1990)	**10**	-2	0	-2	8	8
Burkina Faso I (1991)	**10**	0	0	0	10	10
Jordan (1992)	**10**	0	0	0	10	10
Tanzania (1991)	**9**	-4	-1	-1	5	5
Poland (1991)	**9**	-1	0	-1	8	7
Mauritania (1992)	**9**	0	0	0	9	9
Panama (1992)	**8**	-4	-1	-1	4	8
Mali (1992)	**8**	-3	-1	0	5	5
Lesotho (1991)	**8**	0	0	0	8	8
Philippines (1991)	**8**	0	0	0	8	8
Sri Lanka (1991)	**7**	-5	-1	-2	2	2
Nepal (1992)	**7**	-4	-1	-1	3	3
Zambia (1992)	**7**	-3	-1	0	4	4
Benin (1993)	**6**	-3	-1	0	3	6
Equatorial Guinea (1993)	**5**	-2	0	-2	3	3
Argentina (1992)	**5**	0	0	0	5	4
Sierra Leone (1992)	**5**	0	0	0	5	4
Jamaica (1992)	**4**	-1	0	-1	3	3
Mongolia (1993)	**3**	0	0	0	3	3
Peru (1993)	**3**	0	0	0	3	3

Source: IMF staff estimates.
[1]The methodology of combining NTB coverage and average import tariffs into an overall index of trade restrictiveness is described in Appendix I. Each program's effectiveness date is indicated in parentheses.

viewed was mixed (Table 2).[18] The average targeted improvement in restrictiveness was slightly less than 2 points on the 10-point scale, with a range of zero to 5 points (Figure 2). Almost one-third of the 28 programs (9 programs) did not target an improvement in openness large enough to register on the 10-point scale; 8 programs targeted an improvement of 1–2 points; and 11 programs targeted an improvement of 3 or more points.[19]

Programs supported by Fund arrangements generally targeted at least some reduction in tariff protection, but in many cases these were modest. Slightly more than one-third of programs targeted a reduction in tariffs sufficient to change the classification of tariff protection. Regarding NTBs, slightly more than one-half of programs targeted a reduction sufficient to lower the classification of the restrictiveness of NTBs.

The sequencing of trade reform in these programs generally first targeted NTBs, which was followed or accompanied by a reduction in tariff protection. For the 18 programs in the restrictive classifications, 13 targeted movement toward more liberal regimes, and 11 of those 13 incorporated a reduction in NTB classification; only 2 of the programs with these countries targeted tariff reform alone. This indicates that Fund programs generally focused initially on removing NTBs as the most distortionary element of the trade system.

End of Program Outturns

The overall openness of the trade systems at the conclusion of the programs reviewed is summarized in Figure 3. The number of countries in the restrictive category declined by one-third, from 18 to 12 and a

[18]In assessing the program objective for trade liberalization, all measures targeted during the program were taken into account, including prior actions as well as measures specified after the arrangement went into effect; for example, as part of the second- or third-year programs.

[19]In principle, the index could understate the degree of liberalization targeted, for example, in the most restrictive trade regimes, when changes are introduced, which might be considered an important first step toward longer-term liberalization but are insufficient to move the country below the highly restrictive category. In practice, however, this was rarely the case.

Figure 2. Targeted Change in Overall Restrictiveness

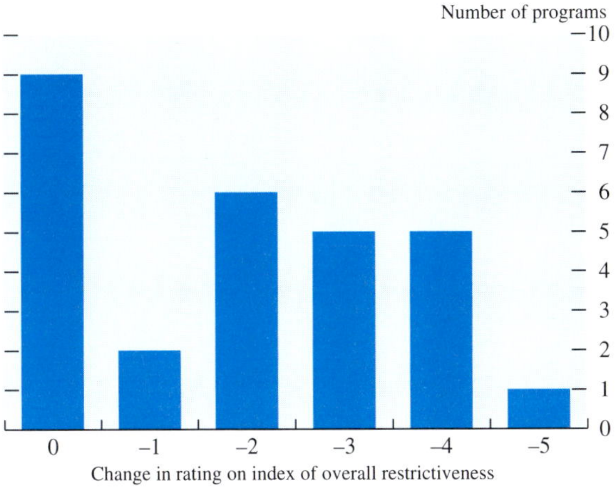

Source: IMF staff estimates.

Figure 3. Initial, Targeted, and Final Distribution of Overall Trade Restrictiveness

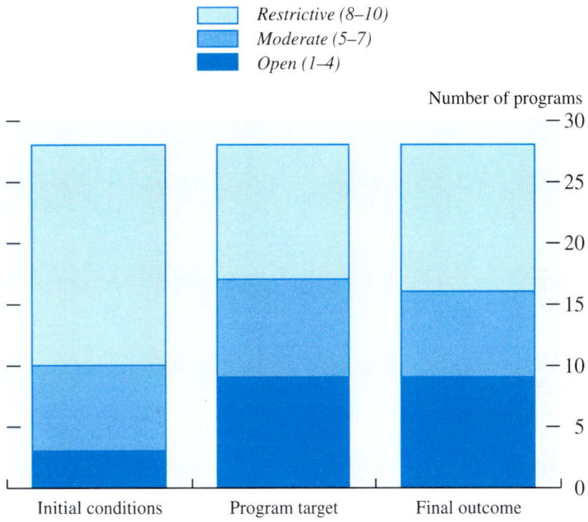

Source: IMF staff estimates.

corresponding increase occurred in the open category. The average actual movement along the 10-point scale was slightly less than 2 points. However, the extent of trade liberalization varied considerably, with a broadly even division between those with no change in overall trade restrictiveness; an improvement by 1 or 2 points; and an improvement by 3 points or more. In four cases, countries liberalized more than targeted under the program, or liberalized unilaterally if the program did not contain trade policy targets. Actual liberalization was less than targeted under the program in only three cases.

Reductions in overall restrictiveness were due to reductions in both tariff and NTBs.[20] Ten of the 28 programs reviewed included lowering tariff protection sufficiently to lower the index classification; in 8 of these cases the targeted reduction was achieved. Moreover, although not directly reflected in the index, progress was made in reducing maximum tariffs and exemptions, hence reducing tariff dispersion. Average tariffs were reduced significantly in two cases but still remained very high, so that tariff protection remained classified as restrictive. In three cases, the envisaged reduction in the level of tariff protection was not achieved. A reduction in tariff exemptions was achieved in 7 programs.

Program objectives for reducing NTBs were somewhat more extensive; 15 of the 28 programs reviewed included targeting a reduction in NTB classification. In 13 of these 15 cases, the targeted reduction was achieved. At the end of the arrangement period there were only 5 cases that had the most restrictive categorization of NTBs, compared with 14 at the beginning. On the other hand, of the 18 programs in the restrictive category, which by definition had the highest level of NTBs, 7 did not target NTB liberalization sufficient to lower the restrictiveness classification.

Targeting, Monitoring, and Overall Results

The review found that Fund programs were successful in achieving the targeted change in the trade regime. As shown in Figure 4, in three-fourths of the programs reviewed, the envisaged outcome was achieved, and in a further 14 percent it was exceeded (although it should be noted that these results include the one-third of programs that did not target any change in restrictiveness). This result was equally true for targeted import tariff and NTB liberalization. As most programs targeted some quantifiable change in restrictiveness, and these targets were generally achieved, the aggregate stance of trade policy in the countries reviewed improved markedly.

To an extent, the success in attaining program targets reflects appropriate use of monitoring, namely, prior actions, performance criteria, structural benchmarks, and reviews. As illustrated in Figure 5, binding monitoring[21] of at least one trade liberalization

[20]Some instances of temporary increases in protection during the program period were eliminated by the end of the program.

[21]Prior actions, performance criteria, benchmarks, and reviews.

Figure 4. Overall Trade Liberalization, Final Outcome Versus Program Objectives[1]

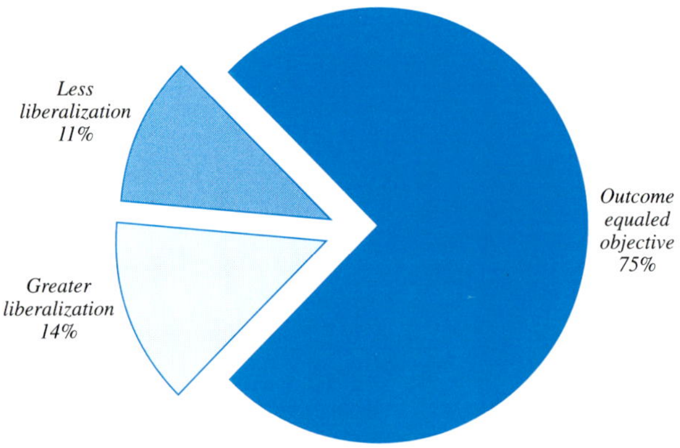

Source: IMF staff estimates.
[1]Includes cases where there was no targeted change in the restrictiveness rating.

Figure 5. Monitoring Instruments Used in Fund Programs

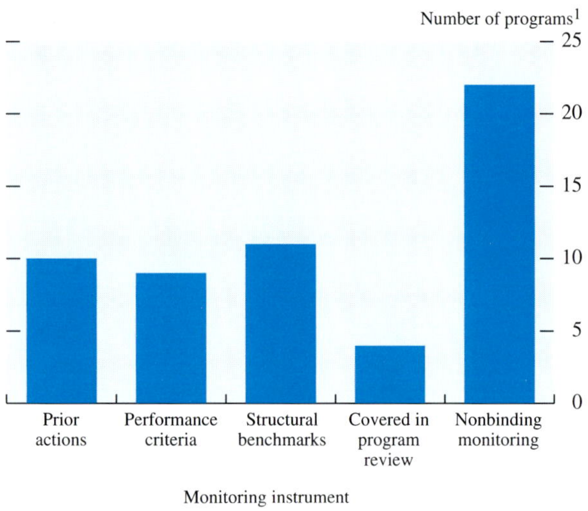

Source: IMF staff estimates.
[1]Multiple instruments may have been used in a program.

measure was used in 23 of the 28 programs and implemented on time in nearly three-fourths of the cases. Of the measures not subject to such monitoring, about half experienced problems with delayed implementation.

Another notable conclusion of the review is that although some statement regarding medium-term trade liberalization was mentioned at the outset in two-thirds of the arrangements, it was generally insufficiently comprehensive or detailed to permit monitoring of the implementation, either in terms of specificity of targets or implementation dates.[22] They were generally not supported by intermediate steps to measure progress in phasing in the targeted liberalization, nor by other nontrade measures that would support the liberalization, such as developing alternative tax revenue sources. These results suggest that trade policy implementation could have been strengthened by placing more emphasis on clearly defined, quantifiable, and monitorable medium-term policy objectives and targets at the beginning of the arrangement. The case studies suggest that this might be further strengthened by the early public announcement of the medium-term targets.

Program Ambitiousness

The following subsections set forth some general observations and factors that may be considered in making judgments about ambitiousness of trade reform and try to assess the ambitiousness of the programs reviewed.

General Principles

The objective of medium-term structural adjustment programs should be to move toward an open trade system characterized by the absence of quantitative restrictions and other NTBs (except for health and security reasons) and low, relatively uniform tariff protection, applied in a transparent and evenhanded manner. Indeed, movement from restrictive to open categories, as measured by the index, means the progressive elimination of NTBs for controlling trade, and reducing tariff protection to low levels by comparison with all Fund members. However, the speed with which this objective should be accomplished is an inherently difficult issue. In principle, such movement should be undertaken as rapidly as possible, but in practice judgements will need to be made on a case-by-case basis, taking account of the particular circumstances of the country concerned.

Clearly a major element determining the pace at which reform should be pursued would be the country's initial conditions. Trade regimes that are more restrictive at the outset incur higher costs from trade distortions and hence need stronger trade liberalization efforts. Economic principles would seem to indicate that, in sequencing trade reform, one should first target the most distortionary aspects of the trade regime, namely, NTBs, in tandem with other reforms. In addition to reaping the benefits from reducing distortions,

[22]Examples include medium-term targets that sought to "rationalize the tariff structure" or "reduce the number of products subject to restrictive licensing" without specifying the extent or details of reform envisaged or the implementation dates.

the tariffication of NTBs almost invariably increases revenue, as discussed below.

The experience of countries that have achieved markedly improved trade and economic growth performance through the adoption of liberal outward-looking policies is also instructive. The experience of four such "good practice" countries, Chile, Colombia, New Zealand, and Singapore, is reviewed in Box 5.[23] These countries made steady and sustained progress in moving from the restrictive to open categorization over a period of about seven to ten years (Figure 6). Their experiences, and the results of the review and the case studies below, confirm that far-reaching trade reform is almost inevitably a long-term process. This highlights the need to avoid policy slippages en route,[24] which would make the eventual success of reform and reaping its economic benefits an even more drawn-out process. It also underlines the fact that, for countries with Fund-supported programs, the reform efforts directed toward the goal of openness may need to be viewed as a continuous process over more than one medium-term arrangement. Both of these factors underscore the need for specified and monitorable medium-term trade targets to be included in the initial objectives of arrangements. The relatively long-term nature of successful reform reinforces the need for close Fund-Bank collaboration, as the intensity of the Fund or the Bank's separate involvement may not be even over the full period of the trade reform effort.

The need for commitment to liberalization on the part of the authorities also underscores the importance of dealing with the nontrade considerations that may constrain trade liberalization on a medium-term basis. As noted above, these include the real or perceived fiscal constraints, administrative capacity, particularly of tax administration, the short-term adjustment costs and disruption involved in any reallocation of economic resources, and the lobbying and rent seeking that are so often associated with trade-related activities.

Assessing the Programs Reviewed

Given the above considerations, it is difficult to translate the range of the trade liberalization objectives of the programs covered by the review into a general assessment of the ambitiousness of medium-term Fund-supported programs. Clearly a number of programs targeted far-reaching and extensive trade reform; the trade reform objectives of Sri Lanka's 1991 ESAF, for example, were ambitious by any standards, as were the reforms targeted in a significant number of other programs. However, if the goal of progressive movement toward an open trade regime is accepted, then many programs may also be characterized as clearly unambitious. In particular, almost one-third of the total did not target a quantifiable reduction in trade restrictiveness, as measured by the index.[25] Excluding the programs of the three countries classified as having open regimes, 28 percent of countries did not target a reduction in restrictiveness. Also, as shown in Table 3, programs in countries classified as restrictive at the outset of the program were not more ambitious in targeting trade reform than programs in countries classified as moderate. In fact, the extent of trade reform targeted was on average less for restrictive than for moderate regimes, and the proportion of programs that targeted no quantifiable trade reform was the same for both categories. This may reflect the fact that highly restrictive countries are those that have resisted liberalization more strongly.

On balance, the findings of the review indicate that, notwithstanding the difficulties of judging the ambitiousness of trade reform efforts, a substantial number of programs targeted and achieved extensive trade reform. However, more liberalization of the trade system should probably have been targeted in a significant number of Fund-supported programs, and particularly in those countries with initially restrictive regimes.

Factors Affecting the Implementation of Trade Reform

The review identified the prevalence of a number of factors that might be expected to hinder or promote trade reform. These focus particularly on fiscal considerations as well as the balance of payments, but also include longer-term Fund involvement during 1990–96, World Bank involvement, the impact of the WTO and other international organizations, and regional trade arrangements. The impact of these factors on program design and implementation is discussed in more detail in Section IV.

Not all factors affecting reform, most significantly "ownership" and political economy constraints, could be considered in the review. Other related factors that can constrain trade reform include lack of an adequate social safety net, supply constraints for countries with undiversified economies or inadequate physical infrastructure, and concerns about the effects of trade reform on unemployment and the impact of openness on consumption patterns and income distribution. While critically important to the design, pace, and implementation of reform, the political economy of trade liberalization is beyond the scope of this study (Box 3).

[23]These countries are illustrative of highly successful open economies and are not necessarily typical of all successful trade-oriented economies.

[24]The issue of slippages in trade policy reforms over the medium term is not addressed in the review. However, the case studies investigated trade reform efforts over a seven-year period and found only limited indication of slippages.

[25]The review found no obvious common thread in these programs that could explain the lack of movement in trade restrictiveness.

Box 5. Trade Policies in Selected "Good Practice" Countries

This box provides some benchmarks for trade reform by looking at four countries known to have open or "good practice" trade policies and with a variety of experiences. The countries, Chile, Colombia, New Zealand, and Singapore, are examples of reformers with strong export growth and economic performance. Their trade regimes have been classified according to the 10-point scale from 1984 to 1996[1] and Figure 6 illustrates how they have opened their trade regimes during that period. Open trade regimes have been a major factor in the strong trade and growth performances of the good practice countries. During 1986–95 their annual export growth averaged 13 percent, while real GDP growth averaged 5 percent. New Zealand's growth record is the most striking—growth shifted from about 1 percent a year to as high as 6 percent after the trade and other major reforms, although some of the increase may be due to cyclical factors.

Chile is often cited as an example of a successful trade reformer. During the 1980s, it virtually eliminated NTBs. Tariffs, which had earlier been increased in response to external shocks, were progressively reduced to a uniform rate of 11 percent.[2] The share of imports facing NTBs during 1991–93 was just 0.1 percent.

When Colombia started reforms in 1984, over 80 percent of its imports required permits, while imports of some 800 products were prohibited and tariffs averaged near 60 percent. Over the next decade, NTBs were virtually eliminated and the average tariff was reduced to under 12 percent.

In Singapore, the proportion of tariff lines covered by NTBs was reduced to 1 percent in the late 1980s and to less than ½ of 1 percent in the early 1990s. Singapore's tariffs have averaged less than 1 percent since 1980.

In 1984, New Zealand's tariffs averaged 16 percent and most imports were subject to restrictive import licensing. By 1993, NTBs applied to less than ½ of 1 percent of imports, and tariffs had been cut to 8.5 percent, with continuing reductions programmed to reduce the average to 3.0 percent in 2000.[3]

[1]Background sources for information on tariffs and nontariff barriers were PECC (1995); GATT (1990); GATT (1991); WTO (1996a, 1996b, and 1996c).

[2]Although Chile's average rate is just above the level needed for a rating of 1 under the 10-point classification, the uniform tariff is likely much less distortive than some other tariff regimes with an average tariff several percentage points below Chile's.

[3]New Zealand's 1996/97 tariffs averaged 6.2 percent.

Balance of Payments and Fiscal Considerations

Meaningful and sustainable trade reform needs to be developed as part of a coherent package of structural and macroeconomic policy reforms.[26] Fiscal and balance of payments positions are central to the macroeconomic framework, and appropriate exchange rate policies are an integral part of Fund-supported programs. Balance of payments concerns may influence the extent and pace of trade liberalization, particularly if appropriate exchange rate policies are not adopted and if existing restrictions are thought to be needed to manage the balance of payments position to preserve macroeconomic stability.[27] In the review, balance of payments difficulties were cited explicitly only once, in connection with the introduction of a temporary measure that increased the restrictiveness of the trade regime. There was no evidence that exchange rate considerations directly influenced the extent of trade reform commitments or implementation.

Fiscal policy concerns[28] are frequently cited as a reason for delaying trade reform. In practice the fiscal impact of liberalizing the trade system could be positive,

Figure 6. Trade Policies in Selected "Good Practice" Countries

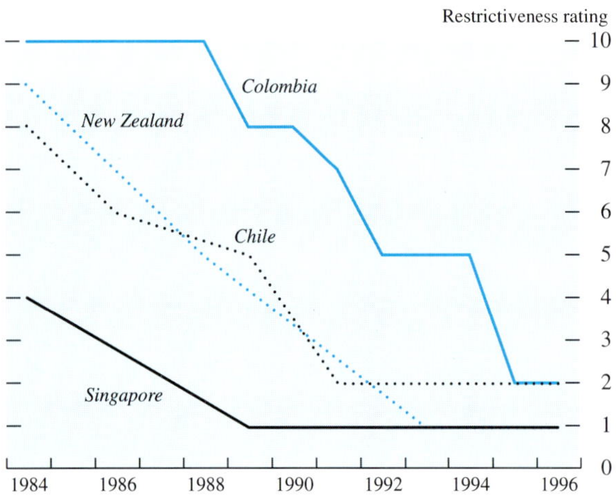

Source: IMF staff estimates.

[26]Kirmani and others (1994b.)

[27]Under WTO rules, member countries have recourse to balance of payments safeguards, that is, provisions permitting member countries to impose temporary restrictions on trade in goods and services for balance of payments purposes.

[28]The analysis of this section is based on reviews of the literature, on Fund and Bank staff experiences, particularly Fund staff's reviews of tax policy and administration, and on the review of Fund arrangements included in this study.

Table 3. Ambitiousness of Programs Reviewed

Initial Classification	Number of Programs	Average Targeted Change in Index	Programs That Targeted No Change in Overall Restrictiveness
Restrictive	18	2.0	5 (28 percent)
Moderate	7	2.4	2 (29 percent)

Source: IMF staff estimates.

negative, or neutral, depending on the reforms introduced and the specific circumstances of the country concerned. It should be noted that in the context of Fund programs the ratio of trade taxes to GDP may increase during trade reform, because of factors such as exchange rate changes, increases in the import-to-GDP ratio (including the impact of increased donor financing), and improvements in tax and customs administration. Although lowering the average tariff in a system with already low or moderate tariff rates will, other things being equal, generally reduce revenue,[29] at least in the short term, the fiscal impact of most other aspects of trade reform is likely to be positive or ambiguous (Table 4). Tariffication of QRs and other NTBs on imports or exports will improve government finances, possibly significantly, as will the elimination of tariff exemptions (excluding export duty drawback schemes) and trade-related subsidies.[30] Reductions in very high tariffs may also increase fiscal revenue, if the effect of expanded imports outweighs the reduced tax rate.[31] Simplification of the tariff system through a move to more uniform rates or a reduction in the number of rates may also tend to increase fiscal revenue through increased transparency and simplification of tax administration. Even lowering export taxes may, in some circumstances, have a positive impact on revenue, depending on the extent and speed with which it expands total trade and reduces illegal activity such as smuggling.

The net fiscal impact of trade reform will depend crucially upon the mix of elements in the trade reform package, as well as the countries' initial circumstances. Clearly the above argues for the early focus of trade reform to be broad based and to include the likely positive revenue elements. Papageorgiou, Michaely, and Choksi (1991), World Bank (1992), and Thomas, Nash, and others (1991) each examined individual country cases from the 1970s and 1980s and found that trade reform may well be associated with an increase in revenue from import taxes when elimination or tariffication of nontariff barriers is an important focus of the trade reform.

Even if a first-round revenue loss from trade reform is anticipated, a preferred policy response would be to increase revenues from other less distorting, broader-based taxes,[32] such as value-added taxes (VATs) applied equally to imports and domestic production.[33] Optimal tax theory starts with the objective of raising revenue with the least economic distortion.[34] A tariff is an inefficient tax that tends to raise prices on both imports and their domestic substitutes while only collecting revenue on imports. The distortion to the economy from taxing both imports and domestic substitutes at equivalent tax rates is generally less than that of taxing imports alone, and the revenue yield is greater from taxing both.[35]

Tax administration concerns also favor tariff reform in spite of the low cost of administering trade taxes relative to the revenue; this is true both because many elements of tariff reform simplify tax administration by reducing evasion or eliminating exemptions and also because the broader-based alternative tax sources generally increase collected revenue, with less economic distortion. Many of the prescriptions for trade reforms, particularly low, relatively uniform tariffs with few exemptions and an absence of NTBs, tend to make revenue collection more efficient through simplification and transparency. Fund tax policy advice has generally advocated simple tax rate structures with low rates and broad-based application, recognizing that overly complicated tax systems tend to generate inefficiencies, high compliance costs, tax evasion, and rent seeking.

Nevertheless, there are some fiscal arguments for gradualism in trade reform. Trade taxes may be an important source of fiscal revenue, particularly in low-income countries (see Stotsky, 1995). At some point in the process of tariff reduction, further reduction always lowers revenue, at least in the short run. To the extent trade taxes account for a significant part of fiscal revenue and total revenue is low, fiscal considerations may be an important factor in the design and pace of trade reform, particularly regarding lowering average tariffs. A shift to a

[29]If the average tariff is very high, however, the impact of a reduction may be ambiguous.

[30]Rajapatirana (1996) assessed the impact of trade policies in Latin America in the 1970s and 1980s and found three cases in which trade liberalization, largely through liberalization of quantitative restrictions, resulted in an increase in revenue from trade taxes (Chile, Colombia, and Costa Rica).

[31]Nogués and Gulati (1992, p. 70) found that in Chile, reductions in very high tariffs were associated with increases in tariff revenue and found "no evidence that higher tariff protection is associated with higher tariff and tax revenues" in a sample of five Latin American countries.

[32]Throughout the study, it is assumed that trade reform should not affect the overall fiscal policy stance, which is set to achieve savings and investment objectives consistent with targeted growth and inflation.

[33]From a trade perspective, a VAT may be preferable to a cascading sales tax since the latter tends to discriminate in favor of imports and against exports.

[34]Dixit (1985) provides a detailed explanation of the application of optimal tax theory to taxes on international trade.

[35]This is an important source of efficiency gains, because economic distortions tend to increase more than proportionately with increases in tax rates.

Table 4. Fiscal Impact of Trade Reform Elements

Trade Reform	Expected Fiscal Impact
Reduce moderate or low average tariff	Negative
Reduce high average tariff	Ambiguous
Lower maximum tariff	Ambiguous
Reduce tariff dispersion	Ambiguous/positive
Replace quantitative restrictions with tariffs and liberalize other nontariff barriers on trade	Positive
Eliminate tariff exemptions	Positive
Eliminate trade-related subsidies	Positive
Eliminate state trading monopolies	Ambiguous/positive
Eliminate export taxes	Ambiguous/negative

Sources: IMF and World Bank staff estimates.

broader-based tax, such as a VAT, will reduce reliance on trade taxes, but generally requires careful preparation. Further, a country may have difficulty collecting taxes because of an overly complex tax system, lack of effective sanctions for tax offenders, lack of trained personnel, tax avoidance and evasion, and generally weak administrative capacity (Faria and Yücelik, 1995). In these cases, technical assistance to improve the efficiency of tax administration and increase enforcement should probably precede implementation of substantial trade tax reforms that are likely to reduce fiscal revenues.

In addition, to the extent that adjustment programs tend to be introduced in countries with relatively weak and undiversified fiscal systems and large fiscal imbalances, mobilizing alternative revenue sources and diversifying tax sources away from trade taxes may be a longer-term project, which also argues for technical assistance at an early stage. In these cases, however, there is still no reason to delay implementation of trade reform elements that increase revenue or are revenue neutral. Indeed, the difficulties in collecting more efficient taxes strengthen the case for proceeding rapidly with the revenue-increasing elements of trade reform, particularly the tariffication of QRs and other NTBs and curtailing exemptions.

With regard to the impact of fiscal considerations in undertaking the trade reforms for the countries covered by this review, the fiscal conditions likely to present the most difficulties would include relatively heavy dependence on trade taxes, relatively low revenues in relation to gross domestic product (GDP), and a weak overall fiscal position. On this basis, the review included four indicators to assess initial fiscal conditions: (1) the ratio of trade taxes to total taxes; (2) the ratio of trade tax revenue to GDP; (3) the ratio of tax revenue to GDP; and (4) the targeted change in the ratio of budget deficit to GDP.

The results for these indicators are summarized in Figure 7. As can be seen, a direct relationship between the initial fiscal conditions and the ambitiousness of trade reform targeted, including for the ratio of trade taxes to total taxes, is not evident for the programs reviewed. Only five cases were found in which the initial fiscal conditions may have been expected to act as a constraint to trade reform. In those cases, countries lacked a VAT and at least two of the three conditions of high dependency on trade taxes—low revenue effort and large targeted reduction in the budget deficit—were satisfied.[36] Despite these adverse initial conditions, three of these countries targeted and implemented trade reform of at least 3 points on the 10-point scale, and the other two countries targeted and implemented trade reform of 2 points. The evidence available in this review, albeit limited, indicates no direct relationship between fiscal conditions and trade reform objectives and that trade reform should not necessarily be ruled out because of a backdrop of difficult fiscal circumstances. Moreover, while it is beyond the scope of this study to assess the availability of alternative revenue sources and other fiscal actions, the review indicated that exemptions were noted as a problem in at least half of the cases, state trading monopolies in more than half the cases, and as indicated above, NTBs were prevalent throughout. Moreover, the evidence from the case studies, while also limited, suggests that more attention could have been given to fiscal policies that would support trade reform.

Nevertheless, the problems posed by introducing trade reform should not be minimized, particularly in cases where that reform is perceived as likely to have negative first-round fiscal implications. Even if alternative revenue sources or expenditure restraints appear to be readily available, action in these areas is likely to pose its own political and economic challenges. Moreover, the consideration of fiscal alternatives will be in the context of program design, which usually involves fiscal pressures in many areas of both revenue and expenditures, including outlays in support of structural reforms other than trade policy. This underlines the importance of introducing broad-based trade reform programs that include, at an early stage, elements such as the tariffication of QRs and other NTBs, reduced exemptions and trade-related subsidies as well as early technical assistance to broaden the tax base and improve tax administration.

Longer-Term Fund Involvement During 1990–96

As noted above, the review provides a snapshot of trade reform in Fund-supported programs rather than a comprehensive analysis in the context of Fund relations with countries over a longer period. Such longer-term involvement in fact characterizes the great majority of the arrangements covered in the review. This raises issues

[36]Fiscal conditions are considered as a possible constraint on trade reform if trade taxes were a high proportion of total taxes (over 30 percent), tax revenue was low (less than 10 percent of GDP), the targeted reduction in the budget deficit over the period of the arrangement was high (over 4 percent of GDP), or if there was no broad-based consumption tax such as a VAT. These cutoff levels were based on a review of data for developing countries and Fund programs.

Figure 7. Initial Fiscal Indicators for the Programs Reviewed

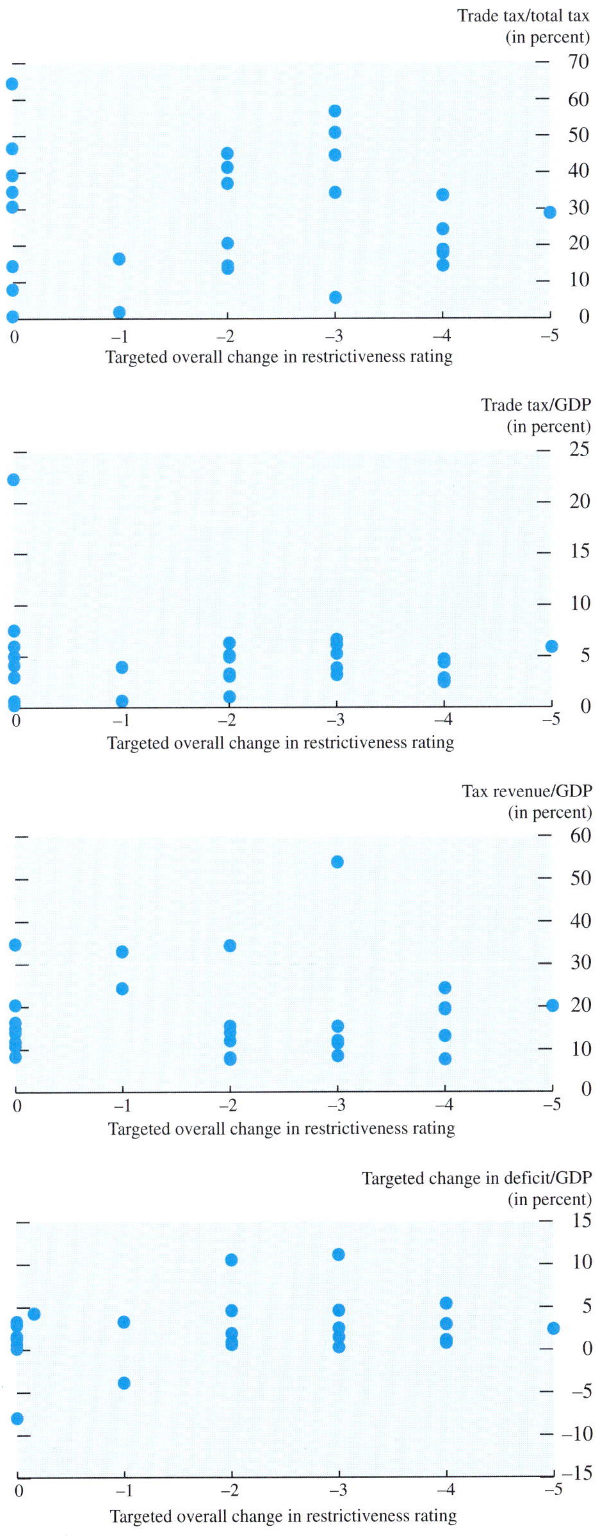

Source: IMF staff estimates.

about the degree of liberalization included in any single program, the sequencing and timing of trade reform with other program measures in a longer-term context, and the need for continued steady progress in trade reform. Figure 8 shows all arrangements during the 1990–96 period for each country included in the study. As can be seen, for only two countries (the Comoros and Zimbabwe) was the program reviewed the only one supported by the Fund during the period. Twenty-one programs were followed by a successor arrangement,[37] and 20 were preceded by an arrangement. In 15 cases, there was both a preceding and successor arrangement.

On the basis of this longer-term Fund involvement, some might argue that broad macroeconomic imbalances should be vigorously addressed at the outset, with important structural reforms, including trade reforms, addressed extensively in subsequent programs. This does not appear to have been the case in the countries reviewed. First, the initial degree of restrictiveness of the trade regimes of countries that had completed earlier Fund arrangements was similar to that of the entire sample of programs reviewed. Thus, on the basis of the information available in this study, prior arrangements during 1990–96 do not appear to have promoted a start to the reform process. Second, trade liberalization objectives for countries that had already completed Fund arrangements were about the same as in other programs, that is, completion of an earlier arrangement did not lead to trade reform being addressed more extensively in the subsequent arrangement. In contrast, it may be noted that the good practice countries moved steadily from the restrictive to open category, with reform efforts sustained throughout the entire adjustment period. These findings are tentative, as only a short period was surveyed. Nevertheless, they underscore the need for steady and sustained progress to reach the objective of a liberal trade regime.

World Bank Involvement, the WTO, and Other International Organizations

The World Bank's involvement was cited in three-fourths of the programs reviewed as a factor that influenced trade reform. In two-thirds of the cases, the Bank's involvement took the form of loans with trade conditionality, and in the remaining cases it took the form of policy advice, combined with technical assistance. The available information provided limited insight into the modalities of the Fund-Bank collaboration and whether it had any impact on the degree of program ambitiousness. However, in the review and also in the case studies in Section IV, there was no indication of differences of view. Further, as noted above, the implementation record of agreed objectives is strong. This suggests that the results of Fund and Bank collaboration in trade policy have

[37]The ESAF for Bangladesh was followed by a program monitored by the IMF staff under enhanced surveillance.

Figure 8. Arrangements Included in the Review[1]

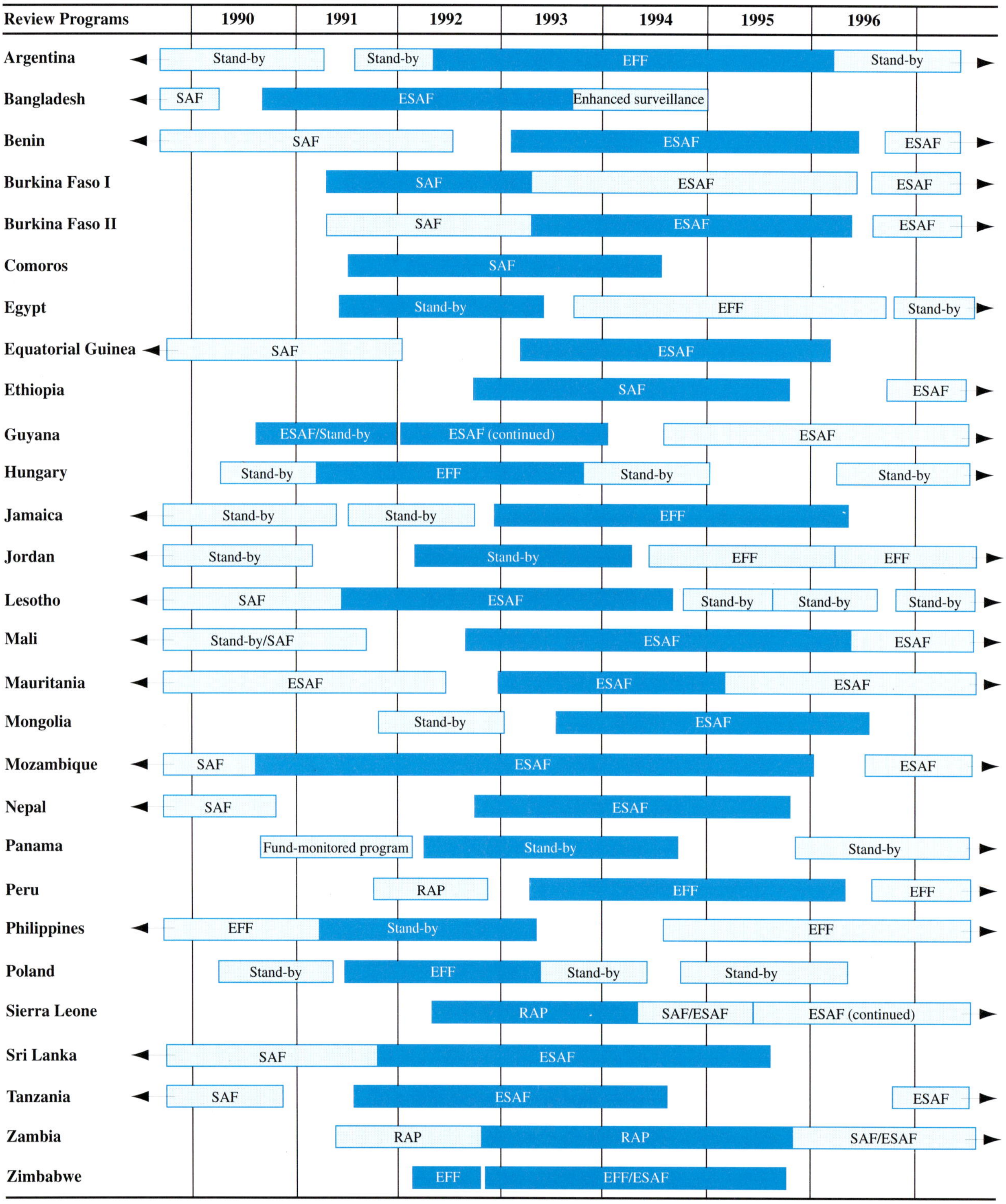

Source: IMF, *Transactions of the Fund Yearbook.*

[1]Programs shaded solid blue were included in the review portion of the study. See text for selection criteria and List of Abbreviations. Where overlaps occur, the period of the later arrangement is shown.

been effective in achieving the results targeted but leave open the question as to whether joint involvement increases the ambitiousness of the reform effort.

Trade liberalization by Fund members that is linked to the WTO results from either negotiations on WTO accession or implementation of multilateral commitments. The accession process can take several years and the liberalization linked to accession may be phased over a similar period.[38] In the programs reviewed, the WTO was cited as affecting the degree of trade liberalization in three cases; in two, implementation of certain trade measures was part of the countries' liberalization obligations under WTO agreements; and in the other, trade liberalization was linked to WTO accession. Hence, the effect of WTO obligations appears to have been limited for the programs reviewed. Interaction with other international organizations was limited to two instances where regional development banks were mentioned as having a modest influence on trade liberalization.

Regional Trading Arrangements

Regional trading arrangements (RTAs) are numerous and can play an important role in a country's trade policy stance (Box 6). IMF staff have, with few exceptions, taken up trade reform issues with the individual RTA members rather than on a regional basis, even in the case of customs unions.

In practice, membership in an RTA has served either to promote or inhibit the trade liberalization of individual countries, depending on whether a country's trade liberalization objectives are more or less ambitious than those of its RTA partners and whether the RTA constrains unilateral action by members setting common external tariffs and other trade policies, as is the case for customs unions. If the objectives of the RTA are progressive in relation to the initial position of its members, it may promote more rapid liberalization than might otherwise occur (as appears to have been so with Guyana and Jamaica in this review). In other cases, such membership may have acted as a constraint to trade liberalization. Although cited specifically in only five of the country cases reviewed, the influence of RTAs may be an increasingly important factor in trade policy because of the growing extent and coverage of RTA membership;[39] during 1990–97, so far 62 RTAs were notified to the WTO, compared with only 13 during the 1980s.

[38]IMF staff have usually argued that since WTO accession negotiations involve bindings of maximum rather than applied rates, the WTO accession process should not constrain more ambitious reforms that are economically desirable.

[39]While not cited in the review, Zambia's participation in the Cross-Border Initiative (CBI) has influenced its trade policy, as noted in the case studies below.

Box 6. Regional Trading Arrangements

Regional trading arrangements (RTAs) and other regional trade initiatives are numerous and can play an important role in the trade policy stance of Fund members. The Fund has stressed that nondiscriminatory trade liberalization on a most-favored-nation (MFN) basis is the first-best policy with the ultimate objective being global free trade. RTAs should be implemented in a manner that promotes rather than impedes this objective. The following principles are more likely to result in RTAs that serve as building, rather than stumbling blocks, to multilateral liberalization: (1) the RTA should include all sectors; (2) there should be a short and concrete schedule for full liberalization; (3) substantial external liberalization should precede or accompany preferential liberalization to avoid trade diversion; (4) rules of origin should be transparent, liberal, and uniform; (5) customs unions should strive to adopt low common external tariffs; (6) use of antidumping and countervailing duty actions should be subject to strict disciplines; (7) the economic benefits of RTAs can be enhanced by deeper forms of integration (e.g., liberalization of trade in services); and (8) rules of accession should be liberal.

The WTO rules governing RTAs take account of some of these principles. They specify that substantially all trade in goods between members should be covered by an RTA; external trade barriers to third parties should not be raised; trade barriers within RTA partners should be eliminated within a reasonable period of time; and RTAs should be notified to the WTO. Nearly all WTO members have reported the WTO that they are parties to at least one RTA.

The impact of RTAs on trade policy varies considerably. While trade liberalization on an MFN basis is an important complement to preferential liberalization between RTA members, the modalities for achieving such liberalization pose challenges in the case of customs unions; these challenges are not present in free trade agreements. Customs unions include common external tariffs and other common trade policies that constrain the trade policies of member countries. In this case, the effect of the RTA will depend, inter alia, on whether a country's trade liberalization objectives are more or less ambitious than those of its RTA partners. If the ambitiousness of the RTA's trade liberalization is greater or smaller than that of the individual country, it will quicken or slow, respectively, trade reform of that member country. In contrast, free trade agreements usually include no restrictions on external MFN liberalization.

IV

Case Studies of Trade Policy in Fund-Supported Programs

Based on six detailed case studies, this section expands the analysis of trade reform in Fund-supported programs to cover a longer time period, to include the design and negotiation stages of programs, and to examine more closely the factors influencing program design and implementation. Its objectives are to analyze (1) the trade reform effort over a seven-year period, both within and outside the context of Fund-supported programs; (2) the evolution of program targets and the influence of different factors, particularly fiscal considerations, on program design; (3) the implementation of trade reforms and the factors contributing to or inhibiting the implementation of these reforms; and (4) the elements that may have contributed to successful trade liberalization and the lessons that can be drawn.

The six countries covered by the case studies, Bangladesh, Egypt, Hungary, Sri Lanka, Zambia, and Zimbabwe, were selected from the review in Section III. The selection criteria aimed at a sample that would reflect different trade liberalization outcomes and strong or weak trade policy program content.[40] Account was also taken of other factors such as the availability of information on the trade regimes and geographic diversity. According to the review in Section III, Hungary, Sri Lanka, and Zambia are examples of countries with reasonably strong trade programs that were successfully implemented. Zimbabwe also had a strong program, but implementation was less successful. Bangladesh and Egypt, in the period under review, had less ambitious programs relative to the initial degree of restrictiveness. Trade reform efforts were examined during the entire 1990–96 period. Programs that started in the late 1980s and those currently under way and not yet concluded were also incorporated if they were an integral part of the trade reform process.[41]

The case studies indicate that (1) reviewing the extent of trade reform during 1990–96, rather than in one medium-term arrangement, did not generally reveal significantly more trade liberalization; (2) program targets were scaled down in the design and negotiation stages in about half of the programs; (3) virtually all trade liberalization in the case study countries in the 1990s occurred in the context of Fund programs; (4) fiscal concerns were the main factor cited during the design stage for limiting the scope of trade reform targets, but available indicators of fiscal conditions, and evidence that fiscally more neutral trade policies may have been available, do not readily support these concerns; (5) cooperation and coordination with the World Bank was important; (6) RTAs could influence program design; and (7) quantifiable and preannounced medium-term targets could be important in program implementation.

The following subsections start with an overview of trade liberalization efforts in the case study countries. This is followed by sections on the design and negotiation of trade reform measures and their implementation. Finally, some lessons are drawn from successful programs.

Trade Liberalization in the 1990s

As measured by the index used in this study, all six countries liberalized trade during the 1990–96 period, although to varying degrees (Table 5). Most started the 1990s with relatively restrictive trade regimes. Four were classified initially as 10 on the index of restrictiveness (Figure 9). The most significant trade liberalization was achieved by the two countries (Sri Lanka and Zambia) that did not initially have highly restrictive regimes; both moved from moderate (7) to open categories (2 and 3, respectively) over the seven-year period. Bangladesh and Hungary also achieved significant liberalization, moving from the most restrictive classification (10) to the moderate category (7 and 6, respectively), and Egypt and Zimbabwe moved from an index classification of 10 to 8.

Fund programs played an important role in the trade liberalization achieved in the 1990s. Twelve of the 16 programs with the case study countries during the period included specific trade liberalization targets. As shown in Table 6, virtually all of the changes in trade restrictiveness during the 1990s took place in the context of Fund-supported programs. The change in trade restrictiveness, as measured by the index, varied from

[40]For more details on the selection of country case studies, see Appendix I.

[41]The case studies for each of the six countries are summarized in Appendix II.

Table 5. Targeted Trade Reform in Fund Programs for Case Study Countries

Program	Initial Conditions	Targeted Change	Final Outcome
Bangladesh			
ESAF, 1990[1]	10	–2	8
Enhanced Surveillance, 1993	8	0	8
Egypt			
Stand-By Arrangement, 1991[1]	10	–2	8
EFF 1993	8	–4	8
Stand-By Arrangement, 1996	8	–4[2]	8[3]
Hungary			
Stand-By Arrangement, 1990	10	0	10
EFF 1991[1]	10	–3	6
Stand-By Arrangement, 1993	6	0	6
Stand-By Arrangement, 1996	7	–1	6
Sri Lanka			
ESAF, 1991[1]	7	–5	2
Zambia			
RAP, 1991	7	0	7
RAP, 1992[1]	7	–3	4
ESAF, 1995	4	–1	3
Zimbabwe			
EFF, 1992[1,4]	10	–4	10
EFF/ESAF, 1992[1,4]	10	–4	8

Source: IMF staff estimates.
[1]Program covered in the review (Section III).
[2]Foreseen in 1998.
[3]Outcome as of the end of 1996.
[4]In the case study, these programs were analyzed separately, because they were designed and negotiated at different times, although the trade policy content of these programs was very similar.

a 2-point to a 5-point movement over a seven-year period. All six countries reduced NTBs. All but Egypt and Zimbabwe reduced average tariffs sufficiently to move by one or more categories.

The case studies show that the programs reviewed in Section III captured most of the trade liberalization achieved during 1990–96 in these countries. Changes in the restrictiveness rating were identical in four countries (Egypt, Hungary, Sri Lanka, and Zimbabwe) despite the longer period of analysis. Two countries (Bangladesh and Zambia) implemented further reductions in the overall restrictiveness of the trade regime. Bangladesh's 1990 ESAF-supported program targeted moderate movement in overall trade restrictiveness; the subsequent 1993 program monitored under enhanced surveillance did not target additional quantifiable trade liberalization. Hungary's 1991 EFF program included ambitious reduction in NTBs, yet the subsequent programs did not make significant further progress, as measured by the index, toward an open trade regime. Egypt's 1993 EFF sought to build upon trade reform in the preceding Fund-supported program. It included far-reaching, medium-term trade policy targets in the context of an ambitious program. However, the program as a whole went off track, and trade reform efforts stalled until the 1996 Stand-By Arrangement, which again incorporated far-reaching trade reform efforts, including a number of important prior actions.[42]

Evolution of Program Targets During the Design and Negotiation Stages

This section assesses how trade reform targets evolved and how different trade-related factors influenced program design.

Evolution of Targets

The case studies attempted to determine the extent to which trade reform objectives were diluted before agreement on a program was reached. Analysis of the process of program design and negotiation is complicated because much of the ebb and flow of the discussions is informal and undocumented. This is particularly true of political economy considerations. Nevertheless, the available information indicates that in about half of the 16 programs covered by the case studies, the extent of trade reform initially proposed was scaled back[43] during the design and negotiation stages.

Available information shows that changes in the extent of trade reform targeted in programs during the design and negotiation stages took place mostly in the more ambitious programs. In five of the seven cases in which the final targeted change in restrictiveness of a program was 3 points or greater, the initial design stages envisaged even more extensive liberalization. In programs with less far-reaching targets, there is less evidence of a scaling back of an initially more ambitious program design. While this finding could be interpreted in various ways, it may indicate more give and take in cases where the authorities were more resolute in their commitment to more rapid trade reform. It may also suggest that the extent of resistance increases directly with the extent of liberalization targeted.

Factors Influencing Design and Negotiation of Trade Reform

The design and negotiation of trade reform in the case study programs were influenced by fiscal and balance of payments considerations, the World Bank,

[42]These prior actions are described in Appendix II.[43]The amount of trade liberalization targeted at this stage is difficult to measure on the index of restrictiveness. Therefore, broad assessment is made on trade liberalization proposed in terms of a general reduction in the scope of restrictiveness.

[43]The amount of trade liberalization targeted at this stage is difficult to measure on the index of restrictiveness. Therefore, broad assessment is made on trade liberalization proposed in terms of a general reduction in the scope of restrictiveness.

Figure 9. Case Study Countries: Ratings of Trade Regime Restrictiveness

Source: IMF staff estimates.

the WTO, RTAs, and unemployment and adjustment cost concerns.

Fiscal Considerations

During 1990–96, fiscal issues were cited in at least one program in five[44] of the six case study countries and were among the main reasons given for lowering program trade reform targets during the design and negotiation stages (Table 7). As noted earlier, the fiscal impact of trade reform depends on the specific elements of the program and the initial circumstances of the country concerned. The following will analyze whether the fiscal situation in the countries citing fiscal concerns was severe enough to justify caution and whether program design included more potentially revenue-enhancing measures, such as tariffication of NTBs and curtailment of exemptions, and measures to broaden the tax base. The analysis is intended to shed some light on the links between trade reform and fiscal concerns, rather than as a full analysis of the fiscal impact of trade reform.

In any Fund program, raising additional revenue to help close a deficit by even a point or so of GDP is always difficult. It is therefore not surprising that fiscal policy concerns are frequently cited as a reason for delaying trade reform, and that delays or even reversals in tariff reductions are made in response to revenue shortfall problems. In several of the case studies, fiscal problems were cited as reasons for slower trade reform. But to say that trade reform was slowed because of fiscal concerns is not to say it needed to be slowed because of fiscal concerns. In the case studies where such references were made, little detailed evidence supported these concerns. There was no evidence of arguments being made as to why revenue-neutral measures such as widening the tax and tariff base could not be implemented.[45] Consider some of the case stud-

[44]Even in the sixth country, Sri Lanka, fiscal considerations were cited by the authorities as affecting the pace of implementing trade reform after the ESAF arrangement, although these have not stopped trade reform.

[45]A similar point is made in a recent study of liberalization in Latin America. Primo Braga, Nogués, and Rajapatirana (1997, p. 104) note the substantial liberalization in the region since the mid-1980s but also observe some slowdown or even reversal: "Many countries that faced fiscal deficits recently have raised tariffs. However, it is not at all clear that fiscal adjustment in the form of higher tariffs will help these countries meet revenue targets."

Table 6. Changes in Trade Restrictiveness Ratings in Case Study Countries During the 1990s

	Overall Change in Trade Restrictiveness Ratings	
Country	Total	Fund Programs
Bangladesh	–3	–2
Egypt	–2	–2
Hungary	–4	–4
Sri Lanka	–5	–5
Zambia	–4	–4
Zimbabwe	–2	–2

Source: IMF staff estimates.

ies.[46] Bangladesh and Zambia were the only cases in which most of the indicators pointed to some fiscal constraints (Tables 8 and 9).[47] Bangladesh lacked a VAT, had a high dependency on trade taxes, and had a ratio of low revenue to GDP. Fiscal concerns appear to have been accepted as a constraint to more rapid trade reform in the 1990 program. While average tariffs were reduced, some were increased, and NTB removal was relatively gradual. Many of the indicators for Zambia also point to difficult fiscal circumstances, notably a high dependence on trade taxes, a large fiscal deficit reduction target, and an absence of broad-based consumption taxes. In Zambia, the design of trade reform focused initially on substantial NTB reductions with tariff reform undertaken subsequently as revenues from other sources materialized. In Egypt, Hungary, and Zimbabwe, the targeted reductions in the fiscal deficit were high, but revenue collection was moderate to high and dependence on trade taxes for revenue moderate. In these cases, the fiscal constraints on trade reform appear less stringent. In Zimbabwe, the authorities' fiscal concerns appear to have led to slower NTB removal than initially foreseen, although the linkage is unclear. In Egypt, tariffs were increased for fiscal reasons in 1991, while in Hungary the removal of an import surcharge was slowed down,[48] compared with the initial proposal of the IMF staff, also because of fiscal reasons.

Efforts to address fiscal concerns by designing and sequencing trade reform in a more revenue-neutral way and accompanying it with complementary fiscal measures varied. In Bangladesh, the initial program, while reducing average tariffs, targeted only limited NTB removal, few reductions in exemptions, and only some compensatory revenue measures (Table 10). Whether more could have been done to broaden the trade reform in a revenue-neutral manner is hard to assess. Bangladesh's low collection rates for tariff revenue compared with statutory tariff rates[49] suggest that program design could have paid more attention to exemptions. Furthermore, a faster pace of removing import NTBs might have had a positive revenue impact.[50]

In Zambia, as noted above, fiscal concerns led to an early focus on NTB removal rather than reduced tariff

[46]However, this need not imply that slower reforms were not justified, since other constraints such as political economy factors may have required slower liberalization.

[47]The indicators used were the existence of a VAT, capacity for revenue collection (tax revenue/GDP), dependence on trade taxes for revenue (trade taxes/tax revenue), the targeted reduction in the fiscal deficit/GDP, and the extent of exemptions.

[48]The surcharge, however, was subsequently removed somewhat ahead of the program schedule.

[49]For example, while the average tariff was 89 percent, actual collection of import duties was only 16 percent of imports in 1990. The ratio may be misleading due to the existence of donor-financed (duty-free) imports or an export processing zone, membership in an RTA, and various other factors. Nevertheless, reduction of exemptions to import and sales taxes was stated only as a medium-term target, without any specificity.

[50]The only binding conditionality on trade reform in the initial program was a prior action related to the tariffication of NTBs covering 5 percent of tariff lines, leaving another 20 percent still subject to NTBs.

Table 7. Factors Cited as Influencing Trade Reform for Case Study Countries

Factor	Bangladesh	Egypt	Hungary	Sri Lanka	Zambia	Zimbabwe
World Bank	X_D	$X_{D,I}$	$X_{D,I}$	$X_{D,I}$	$X_{D,I}$	X_D
Fiscal	$X_{D,I}$	X_D	X_D		X_D	X_D
World Trade Organization		X_I	X_D		X_I	
Balance of payments	$X_{D,I}$	X_D	X_D			
Political economy		$X_{D,I}$	X_D		X_I	
Unemployment		$X_{D,I}$	X_D			
Overall program implementation		X_I				X_I
Regional trading arrangement			X_D		X_D	

Source: IMF staff estimates.
Note: D = cited during the design stage of programs; I = cited during the implementation stage of programs.

Table 8. Fiscal Indicators in Countries Where Fiscal Factors Were Cited as Influencing Program Design[1]

Fiscal Issues Cited (Program and Year)	Dependence on Trade Taxes[2]	Revenue Collection[3]	Value-Added Tax	Targeted Deficit Reduction[4]	Extent of Exemptions[5]
Bangladesh (ESAF, 1990)	H	L	No	L	H
Egypt (Stand-By Arrangement, 1991)	M	M	No	H	H
Hungary (Stand-By Arrangement, 1996)	M	H	Yes	H	M
Zambia (RAP, 1992)	H	H	No	H	L
Zimbabwe (EFF/ESAF, 1992)	M	H	No	H	L

Source: IMF staff estimates.

[1]Depending on the time of negotiations, fiscal indicators are from the program year or the preceding year.

[2]Share of trade taxes in total tax revenue. High ≥ 30 percent; Medium = 10–30 percent; Low ≤ 10 percent.

[3]Share of tax revenue in GDP. High ≥ 20 percent; Medium = 10–20 percent; Low ≤ 10 percent.

[4]Change in percent of GDP over a three-year period. High > 4 percent; Low < 2.

[5]Extent of exemptions is measured taking into account the ratio of average tariffs collected to average statutory rates.

protection. At the same time, measures were initiated to diversify the revenue base, including reduced exemptions and discretionary waivers from import taxes, increased sales taxes on domestic goods, and a conversion of the sales tax to a VAT in 1995. These actions effectively paved the way for future tariff reform. In Zimbabwe, trade reform focused largely on liberalization of import licensing related to foreign exchange restrictions and gradual elimination of a 20 percent import surcharge. The fiscal impact of the tariff reform was to be reduced by increasing minimum tariffs and reducing exemptions. However, the program did not foresee introduction of a VAT or other measures to diversify the revenue base.

In Hungary, the phasing out of the import surcharge within the context of the 1996 Stand-By Arrangement was slowed because of fiscal concerns. The program did contain measures to reduce exemptions and diversify the revenue base. However, fiscal concerns could have been further alleviated by the tariffication of import NTBs. In Egypt, tariffs were increased for fiscal revenue reasons in 1991, but only modest targets were set for the replacement of some NTBs by tariffs. A broad-based sales tax was introduced in the program, which was planned later to lead to a VAT. Furthermore, a greater reduction in exemptions from import duties could have been attempted.[51]

While the fiscal impact of trade reform is an important concern of policymakers, the above discussion suggests that in some cases the programs could have targeted more far-reaching trade reform had more attention been given to supporting fiscal policies and to revenue-neutral trade measures. Zambia's ambitious trade reform was the only one that relied on NTB removal and substantial fiscal broadening as a prelude to reducing tariff protection. Also, difficult fiscal circumstances did not prevent Sri Lanka from pursuing ambitious trade reform. The experience of Sri Lanka incidentally also highlights the importance of comprehensive, well-specified medium-term targets for trade reform as part of an overall medium-term policy framework to ensure that supporting measures are implemented, including early provision of appropriate technical assistance.

Balance of Payments

Balance of payments conditions were cited as having affected the formulation of the trade content of Fund-supported programs in Bangladesh, Egypt, and Hungary. In all three countries, it resulted in slower trade reform than initially envisaged. The balance of payments position and its components are determined by a variety of factors other than trade policies, including notably exchange rate, fiscal, and monetary policies. The severity of a country's balance of payments situation depends on these (and other) factors, and whether the balance of payments situation justifies slower trade reform is difficult to judge.[52]

[51]Collection of import duties was about 9 percent of imports while the average tariff was estimated to be about 35 percent in 1990/91.

[52]As a general rule, trade restrictions are not the appropriate policy option for addressing external imbalances, because they add to economic distortions and do not address the cause of the imbalance. This principle underlies the legal foundation of the WTO as well as the Fund's Articles of Agreement. External imbalances should be addressed by appropriate macroeconomic and structural policies that deal with the underlying investment-saving imbalances. The use of trade restrictions can be justified only in exceptional circumstances, and then only as a temporary short-term measure.

Table 9. Case Study Fiscal and Balance of Payments Information

	1990	1991	1992	1993	1994	1995	1996
Bangladesh		ESAF		Enhanced Surveillance			
Trade taxes/total taxes	37.3	36.2	34.5	31.5	31.0	32.9	31.4
Fiscal balance/GDP (incl. grants)	–2.8	–0.6	1.4	0.8	1.0	–0.5	–3.0
Tax revenue/GDP	7.4	7.4	8.3	8.9	8.7	8.8	8.5
VAT exist[1]	No	No	Yes	Yes	Yes	Yes	Yes
Current account balance (percent of GDP) (incl. grants)	–3.4	–0.6	1.4	0.8	1.0	–0.5	–2.8
Reserves (months of merchandise imports)	1.6	3.0	5.5	6.3	7.9	6.3	3.6
Real effective exchange rate (period average)	100.0	98.2	92.3	91.6	88.3	85.9	85.7
Egypt			Stand-by		EFF		Stand-by
Trade taxes/total taxes	24.8	21.1	18.9	18.3	19.5	20.5	20.7
Fiscal balance/GDP (incl. grants)	–15.8	–17.2	–4.2	–3.5	–2.1	–1.3	–1.3
Tax revenue/GDP	14.9	15.7	17.5	17.4	18.1	17.1	17.0
VAT exist[1]	No	No	No	No	No	No	No
Current account balance (percent of GDP) (incl. grants)	–3.4	5.1	8.8	4.6	0.4	0.7	–0.3
Reserves (months of merchandise imports)	3.4	7.2	13.3	17.3	19.7	18.6	16.0
Real effective exchange rate (period average)	100.0	96.6	102.0	117.0	121.2	120.0	128.3
Hungary	Stand-by		EFF		Stand-by		Stand-by
Trade taxes/total taxes	11.0	7.0	8.0	9.0	8.0	11.0	9.0
Fiscal balance/GDP (incl. grants)	0.5	–3.3	–7.2	–7.8	–7.4	–6.6	–3.2
Tax revenue/GDP	44.6	42.3	41.5	42.1	40.4	40.0	40.0
VAT exist[1]	Yes	Yes	Yes	Yes	Yes	Yes	Yes
Current account balance (percent of GDP) (incl. grants)	0.4	0.8	0.9	–9.0	–9.5	–5.6	–3.8
Reserves (months of merchandise imports)	2.3	5.2	5.2	7.1	7.0	9.5	7.0
Real effective exchange rate (period average)	100.0	111.6	120.9	132.1	131.1	125.8	128.0
Sri Lanka				ESAF			
Trade taxes/total taxes	31.6	29.0	28.3	24.2	22.7	20.6	19.4
Fiscal balance/GDP (incl. grants)	–7.8	–9.5	–5.4	–6.5	–9.1	–8.8	–8.9
Tax revenue/GDP	21.2	20.4	20.3	20.3	19.0	20.6	19.0
VAT exist[1]	No	No	No	No	No	No	No
Current account balance (percent of GDP) (incl. grants)	–4.6	–6.2	–4.5	–3.9	–6.4	–5.5	–5.0
Reserves (months of merchandise imports)	1.8	2.7	3.3	5.1	5.0	4.8	4.2
Real effective exchange rate (period average)	100.0	104.8	104.5	106.2	106.5	101.4	110.2
Zambia			RAP		RAP		SAF/ESAF
Trade taxes/total taxes (incl. sales tax/VAT on imports)	36.8	33.1	34.5	34.5	33.1	29.9	32.3
Fiscal balance/GDP (incl. grants)	–7.9	–7.2	–2.1	–4.5	–4.6	–4.8	–0.4
Tax revenue/GDP	21.9	23.5	25.2	19.1	25.1	21.0	18.8
VAT exist[1]	No	No	No	No	No	No	Yes
Current account balance (percent of GDP) (incl. grants)	–10.9	—	–2.6	–2.2	–3.3	–6.1	–6.0
Reserves (months of nonmaize imports)	2.05	2.2	2.4	2.8	2.3	1.7	1.7
Real effective exchange rate (period average)	100.0	93.2	89.5	101.6	98.6	94.6	98.3
Zimbabwe			EFF		EFF/ESAF		
Trade taxes/total taxes	20.2	19.0	27.3	20.7	21.8	18.7	18.9
Fiscal balance/GDP (incl. grants)	–9.2	–7.1	–6.8	–9.1	–5.4	–10.1	–9.7
Tax revenue/GDP	28.5	30.3	33.1	27.6	26.7	25.0	24.4
VAT exist[1]	No	No	No	No	No	No	No
Current account balance (percent of GDP) (incl. grants)	–2.2	–7.1	–10.7	–2.4	–2.3	–3.1	–0.2
Reserves (months of goods and services imports)	1.7	1.7	1.7	3.1	2.5	3.3	3.0
Real effective exchange rate (period average)	100.0	84.0	76.5	79.7	74.2	78.3	84.2

Source: IMF staff estimates.
[1]The definition of a VAT varies from country to country.

In Bangladesh (ESAF, 1990), the authorities feared that faster reform could deplete foreign exchange reserves. A previous lifting of trade restrictions was believed to have contributed to a depletion of international reserves. Together with fiscal concerns discussed above, these concerns may have influenced the pace and nature of Bangladesh's initial trade reform, which included modest QR removal and tariff reform. It was nevertheless noted at the time that the main cause of the current account deficit was expansionary monetary policies. The lack of trade reform in Hungary's 1990 Stand-By Arrangement reflected caution with import liberalization because of concerns about the impact of external disequilibria on creditworthiness.

Whether these concerns were justified is again a difficult question to answer. In all three countries, current account deficits were moderate or high at the start of

Table 10. Existence of Policies to Reduce Fiscal Impact of Trade Reform in Programs Citing Fiscal Concerns

	Tariff Targets[1]	NTB Removal	Reduction in Exemptions	Broadening of Tax Base
Bangladesh (ESAF, 1990)	+/–	Yes	n.a.	Yes
Egypt (Stand-By Arrangement, 1991)	+	Yes	Yes	Yes
Hungary (Stand-By Arrangement, 1996)	n.a.	n.a.	Yes	Yes
Zambia (RAP, 1992)	n.a.	Yes	Yes	Yes
Zimbabwe (EFF/ESAF, 1992)	n.a.	Yes	Yes	n.a.
For reference:				
Sri Lanka (ESAF, 1990)	n.a.	Yes	n.a.	Planned

Source: IMF staff estimates.
[1]Increase (+) or decrease (–); n.a. denotes not applicable.

the programs, while reserves were clearly low only in Bangladesh. In any event, if these concerns were legitimate, there are as noted ways to deal with balance of payments problems other than by imposing trade restrictions. In general, Fund-supported adjustment programs provide (temporary) access to Fund resources in support of appropriate macroeconomic and structural policies designed to address the fundamental causes of external imbalances.

World Bank

IMF collaboration with the World Bank in the trade policy area was cited in all six case studies as having influenced the design of trade reform. Based on information available in the case studies, the two institutions appear to have generally complemented each other and there were no instances of significant differences in views or approach. In some cases (Egypt (Stand-By Arrangement, 1991), Sri Lanka (ESAF), and Zambia (RAP, 1991, RAP, 1992)), it was the Bank that took the lead in the design of trade reform, while in one other case (Egypt's Stand-By Arrangement, 1996), the cooperation worked the other way around.

World Trade Organization

Commitments to WTO (or its predecessor the GATT) were significant in only one case study. During formulation of the 1996 Stand-By Arrangement with Hungary, the authorities argued that further liberalization of tariffs and the removal of certain NTBs should be limited to its Uruguay Round commitments and that unilateral liberalization in the Fund-supported program might weaken its position in international negotiations; IMF staff acceded to the authorities' views. Only small reductions in Hungary's remaining NTBs and tariffs were implemented in 1995–96 as a result of Uruguay Round commitments, because of the slow phase-in of liberalizing textiles and reducing agricultural restrictions under these commitments. On balance, these did not significantly reduce overall trade restrictiveness.[53]

Regional Trading Arrangements

Regional trading arrangements played a role in two case studies. In Zambia, commitments under the CBI influenced the design of trade policy in the 1995 SAF and ESAF.[54] The importance of the initiative and the fact that the Fund and Bank were cosponsors meant that in practice the CBI tended to define the extent of trade liberalization targeted and its timetable. The CBI had a positive influence, as its targets represent substantial trade reform in the regional context.[55] Hungary's strategy has been to pursue liberalization in the context of RTAs—mainly Europe and Central European Free Trade Agreements (CEFTA). While participation in RTAs has led to trade liberalization in Hungary in the regional context, discriminatory (non-MFN) trade liberalization may have led to significant trade diversion.

Unemployment and Adjustment Costs

The expected impact on unemployment was cited in two case study countries as affecting the pace and scope of the trade reform. At the time of negotiating Egypt's 1993 EFF, the authorities favored a more

[53]The Uruguay Round reduced only one component of Hungary's tariff structure and did not offset the new import surcharge that was introduced in 1995. When the Uruguay Round cuts started to be implemented, the average tariff actually increased in Hungary from 18 percent to 22 percent. The Uruguay Round NTB cuts did not change Hungary's NTB import coverage ratio.

[54]Credit should be given to the CBI for trade reform in Zimbabwe, although the Fund-supported programs in the case study preceded the start of the CBI.

[55]The CBI also resulted in trade-enhancing reforms in areas such as investment promotion, reduced procedural impediments, and general efforts to curtail impediments to cross-border trade and investment.

gradual approach to liberalization due to the potential short-run effect on employment at a critical time politically. In 1996, during the preparation of Hungary's Stand-By Arrangement, the need to protect local industry was also mentioned as a reason for not reducing all the remaining NTBs.

The short-term adjustment costs, including unemployment, are always an important concern in program design. Although the direct impact on unemployment may be large in specific sectors or demographic groups; the net benefits of trade reform exceed the costs of adjustment, and the net employment effects (considering new jobs in other industries) are in general far smaller. Inefficiencies in resource allocation may or may not safeguard jobs temporarily in inefficient industries, but this would be at the expense of long-term growth potential and new employment creation. Further, the expected employment impact varies, and it is often difficult to disentangle the effect of trade liberalization from other sources of structural change that affect employment. The literature on trade reform does not point to any strong evidence of large net labor displacements or policy reversals based on employment concerns with trade liberalization (Papageorgiou, Michaely, and Choksi, 1991). Other sources of structural change, such as technology, are often found to be more important. Costs of adjustment may also be influenced by the pace of trade reform. Mussa (1986) has shown that adjustment costs are not necessarily higher if reforms are more rapid and preannounced. Nevertheless, labor displacement is a legitimate concern for policymakers and may call for designing accompanying policies, such as targeted social safety nets, that address the costs of short-term adjustment to more liberal trade.

The design and implementation of trade reform can also be influenced by many other factors such as the status of labor market reform and a variety of political economy factors (Box 3). Flexible labor markets make movement of labor easier between industries, which reduces costs of adjustment associated with trade reform. Price liberalization is also important to transmit the new price signals from freer trade to producers and consumers. The influence of these factors on the success of trade reform depends on the circumstances of each country and may warrant attention in program design with trade reform. A review of the importance ascribed to these factors in Fund programs, however, did not indicate a consistent link between the success of trade reform and the presence of these factors or of measures to address them.

Factors Influencing Implementation of Trade Reform

The results show that targeted trade reform in Fund programs in the case study countries, as in the review countries, was generally achieved. In the two cases (Egypt and Zimbabwe) where trade policy targets were not met, it was because the overall program went off track and most targets were not met, including trade policy. This section analyzes various factors that were cited as influencing the implementation of trade reform in Fund programs.

Program-Related Factors

The type of conditionality used on trade measures in the programs covered by the case studies is shown in Table 11. Binding monitoring of at least one trade liberalization measure was used in all programs with trade policy content. As would be expected, the strength of conditionality was related to the importance of the measure for the program, and it appears to have facilitated implementation. In three cases, only measures subject to binding conditionality were implemented. In Bangladesh, the main measures constituted prior actions and accounted for much of the liberalization achieved in the program. The program for Sri Lanka also had relatively strong conditionality on trade measures, which may have been an important factor in Sri Lanka's successful implementation of trade reform. In Zimbabwe, the performance criterion on the liberalization of the import licensing system was implemented, while the nonbinding commitment to reduce tariffs was not. In the other cases, the nature of conditionality does not appear to have been a factor in implementation. Zambia, with less strong conditionality, nevertheless achieved significant liberalization, and the same is true for Hungary's 1991 EFF program. The latter two case studies would appear to suggest that, while the use of binding conditionality may accompany successful program implementation, a much more important factor was the government's commitment to trade reform and ownership of the program.

There is some evidence that programs with more specific medium-term targets had better implementation records. Further, the preannouncement of policies may have enhanced their implementation. Policies and targets that are specified and preannounced can reduce adjustment costs by enabling producers and workers to anticipate changes, and may also reduce lobbying for continued protection. In the most ambitious case, Sri Lanka, the program initiated in the late 1980s had specified medium-term trade goals, and the major elements were preannounced by the government. The subsequent ESAF-supported program was an extension of this trade reform effort. This gave a clear framework for the government to pursue its goals.

Other Factors

While important in the design and negotiation stages, notwithstanding the potential short-term fiscal impact, macroeconomic factors were not cited as hav-

Table 11. Nature of Trade Conditionality for Case Study Countries

	Prior Actions	Benchmarks	Performance Criteria	Review Clause	Other
Bangladesh					
1990 ESAF	x				x
1993 Enhanced surveillance		x		x	
Egypt					
1991 Stand-By Arrangement	x				x
1993 EFF	x			x	x
1996 Stand-By Arrangement	x			x	x
Hungary					
1990 Stand-By Arrangement					
1991 EFF		x			x
1993 Stand-By Arrangement					
1996 Stand-By Arrangement		x			x
Sri Lanka					
1991 ESAF		x	x		x
Zambia					
1991 RAP					
1992 RAP			x		x
1995 ESAF					x
Zimbabwe					
1992 EFF			x		x
1992 EFF/ESAF			x		x

Source: IMF.

ing had a major impact on trade reform implementation. An exception was Zimbabwe's 1992 EFF-supported program, where a severe drought affected the economy. As noted above, most of the program targets for trade reform were met in the six-country sample and, where they were not, it was in the context of a general program failure. Only in Bangladesh were fiscal and balance of payments concerns cited when committed trade measures were not all implemented in 1992. Whether this was justified is uncertain. However, it can be noted that the fiscal deficit, including grants, was not very high and it improved during the program period between 1990–92. Moreover, dependence on trade taxes declined, revenue collection improved during the period, and a VAT was introduced during the second program year to diversify revenue collection.

Cooperation with the World Bank was cited in all cases to have had an impact on program implementation. In a number of cases, Bank and Fund programs had closely related conditionality. In Egypt, for example, when implementation of the trade content of the Bank's Structural Adjustment Loan was delayed, the measures in the Fund's program were delayed as well. In Bangladesh, trade reform under a Fund program was pursued further under a subsequent Bank program. The fact that virtually all liberalization in the six countries in the 1990s occurred in the context of Fund programs, and many of these were closely coordinated with Bank programs, suggests that Fund-Bank collaboration was important to implementation of trade reform in the countries studied.

Obligations to the GATT/WTO affected implementation in only two programs. Certain WTO rules may constrain implementation of programmed policy actions. In Egypt's 1991 Stand-By Arrangement, after the first review of the program, it was discovered that increasing some (lower rate) tariffs as programmed (to narrow dispersion and raise revenue) would breach some of Egypt's GATT bindings. Egypt requested a waiver of its GATT obligations for the tariff increase already implemented, and the programmed plan to continue increasing the lower tariff rates was abandoned. In Zambia, the modalities of levying the surcharge introduced in 1995 outside the Fund program was influenced by WTO rules (increase in duties versus a new tax).[56] The relatively few cases in which such inconsistencies arose may reflect the fact that in recent years the IMF staff, during the design stage, has given increased attention to ensuring consistency of program measures with the countries' GATT/WTO obligations. Similarly, RTAs did not have much impact on the implementation of targeted trade reform.

Lessons from Successful Liberalizers

This section assesses whether any lessons may be learned from the more ambitious and successful liber-

[56]New border taxes cannot be introduced under WTO rules, while existing tariffs can be increased only within existing bindings.

alizers, such as Sri Lanka and Zambia, and whether they did something different from the other case study countries. The evidence from the case studies is limited, but some cautious conclusions can nevertheless be drawn.

First, reforms in both Sri Lanka and Zambia were a continuation of previous efforts initiated in the late 1980s. This implies that the authorities had already gained the initial political support for liberal trade policies, which is likely to be essential to sustain the reform process. In addition, trade reform seems to have been viewed as a medium-term objective. This was clearly the case in Sri Lanka where the reforms were part of a preannounced package with clear medium-term targets. This gave the right signals to policymakers and private agents, and served as an anchor for adjustment. A medium-term perspective was also evident in the continuity of Zambia's reform efforts.

A closely related issue is the authorities' general commitment to expeditious implementation of liberal market-oriented policies, including trade reform. In both countries political commitment to reform was strong. Additional evidence of the importance of ownership and commitment to liberalization can be seen from Hungary's successful reforms in the early 1990s when trade reforms were implemented despite the overall program going off track.

Successful programs, and especially the Zambia program, were designed in a way to counter fiscal or other concerns raised at the outset. Trade reform initially focused on the removal of NTBs, while potentially revenue-reducing tariff reform was left to a later stage. The initial program was also accompanied by various measures to diversify the revenue base by introducing broader-based taxes and targeting a reduction in exemptions.

Last, the fact that such a substantial proportion of trade reform in the case study countries took place in the context of Fund-supported programs shows the importance of the active involvement of the Fund and the Bank in support of the authorities' commitment to appropriate adjustment policies.

V

Conclusions

Liberal trade policies complemented by appropriate macroeconomic and other structural policies in Fund-supported adjustment programs have an important impact on allocative efficiency and thereby on economic growth. Trade reform also contributes to improved transparency and good governance by reducing incentives for lobbying for trade protection and opportunities for rent seeking and by eliminating administrative discretion. These factors underline the importance of trade reform as a key component of structural adjustment efforts.

The study found that some two-thirds of countries covered by the review started Fund-supported programs with relatively restrictive trade regimes, as measured by the index of restrictiveness. Most programs targeted a marked reduction in trade restrictiveness and the targets were, for the most part, achieved. However, a significant number, including those starting with highly restrictive regimes, did not target any quantifiable change in restrictiveness. The results of the study underline the need to target more substantial trade liberalization as an important objective of Fund-supported programs, and particularly in cases where the regime is restrictive.

With respect to the ambitiousness of trade reform efforts, among the programs reviewed, a significant number targeted extensive trade reform, while others targeted limited or no liberalization. An appropriately ambitious pace of reform depends crucially on country-specific circumstances. However, a number of factors may be seen as relevant to the pace of moving toward an open trade regime. These include the initial degree of restrictiveness of the trade system (particularly, the extent of highly distortionary NTBs), the standard set by the good practice countries that have succeeded in moving from restrictive to open trade regimes over a seven- to -ten-year period, and the nature of the constraints facing the authorities, including nontrade factors such as administrative capacity and short-term adjustment costs. These factors may be used to determine the appropriate pace of reform for countries with restrictive or moderate trade regimes to move to open trade systems, and the extent to which trade liberalization should be frontloaded, including through prior actions, and monitored through binding conditionality. Also, these factors may contribute in determining the sequencing of trade reform measures, for example, on the desirability of designing trade reform so that quantitative restrictions are reduced before tariff reform.

The experience of the case study countries and the good practice countries shows that trade reform is a medium- to long-term process. The longer-term nature of trade reform highlights the importance of well-specified and comprehensive program targets for trade reform. This study found that medium-term targets were generally not detailed enough to permit monitoring of their implementation and often focused on only one or two components of the trade regime. Further, these targets were generally not supported by intermediate steps or nontrade measures that would facilitate their achievement. Well-specified medium-term targets appear to have aided program implementation, in those countries that used them, such as Sri Lanka, as did public preannouncement of the program's medium-term trade reform objectives. This indicates the need for increased emphasis on formulating more specific and detailed medium-term trade reform targets, together with intermediate steps and supporting nontrade measures, and that these should preferably be publicly announced at the start of Fund-supported programs.

Fiscal considerations were the main factor cited as having influenced trade reform objectives during program design and negotiation stages. The review of multiyear Fund arrangements in this study found no direct relationship between the strength of trade reform objectives and achievements and countries' initial fiscal circumstances. The initial fiscal impact of trade reform is not necessarily adverse and will depend on country-specific circumstances and the mix of components in the trade reform package. Certain elements of trade reform are likely to increase fiscal revenue, particularly replacing QRs and other NTBs with tariffs, and eliminating customs duty exemptions and trade-related subsidies. This suggests that trade reform should be as broad based as possible and include these elements in the initial stages of reform. Even where the first-round fiscal effects of trade reform are negative, alternative, less distortionary sources of fiscal revenue should be mobilized to the extent feasible. This also underscores the need for providing appropriate technical assistance at an early stage to facilitate the phasing in of trade liberalization. Indeed, the case studies indicate that some countries facing apparently difficult fiscal circumstances were nevertheless able to liberalize quickly and successfully by designing appropriate supporting reforms.

The study indicates that cooperation with other international organizations, particularly the World Bank, facilitates trade reform. The Bank was involved in the area of trade reform in most of the Fund-supported programs included here and all of the case study countries, and virtually all trade liberalization in the period studied took place in the context of these programs. This underscores the importance of Fund-Bank collaboration in the area of trade policy. Moreover, the Fund has strengthened its collaboration with the WTO to ensure policy consistency between the two institutions with regard to common members. Regional trading arrangements influenced trade reform in some countries covered by the review and the case studies. Moreover, the number of RTAs has been growing rapidly in recent years. Recognizing these factors, the Fund should where appropriate seek to expand its dialogue with regional organizations to cover trade policy.

Appendix I
Methodology

This appendix presents the methodological basis for the review of trade policy in Fund-supported programs, including the selection of Fund arrangements for review, the 10-point scale for classifying the restrictiveness of trade regimes, and the selection of countries for detailed case studies. The approach is also compared with other studies on trade reform in developing countries.

Overview of the Basic Approach

A large number of programs supported by Fund arrangements are reviewed to provide a basis for assessing the ambitiousness of trade reform in Fund-supported programs and the implementation record. The trade regime of each country is examined at the outset of the Fund-supported program and its overall trade restrictiveness is assessed, based on a 10-point scale.

The 10-point classification scheme combines measures of the trade restrictiveness of import tariffs and NTBs. Five ranges are specified for import tariffs, with the lowest range (0–10 percent) being the least restrictive and the highest range (25 percent or over) being the most restrictive. Three categories have been specified for NTBs, ranging from open, to moderate, to restrictive. These categories are based mainly on the number of sectors covered by NTBs (whether NTBs are confined to a few sectors of the economy), on the production (whether they cover entire stages of production) or trade coverage of these barriers, and on their restrictiveness.

The five classifications of import tariffs and three classifications of NTBs yield a 15-cell matrix. Within the matrix the cells were converted to a 10-point scale by assigning a relative ranking, from 1 to 10, representing the overall restrictiveness of the trade regime. The most open import tariff and NTB regimes were assigned the number 1, and the most restrictive tariff and NTB regimes were assigned the number 10.

The ambitiousness of trade reform can be assessed by identifying the trade content of each Fund-supported program and assessing how far along the 10-point scale these measures would have moved the trade regime if fully implemented. The implementation of trade reform is assessed by evaluating the overall restrictiveness of the regime at the end of the program period, again based on the ten-point scale.

A number of other questions are covered in the review of each arrangement. Were specific medium-term targets for trade reform included in the original program? How were different types of monitoring instruments used and how did they influence implementation of trade reform? What was the role of the World Bank in respect of trade reform for the programs covered? What role did the GATT/WTO and other international institutions play? Did membership in an RTA promote or impede liberalization? How did fiscal and balance of payments considerations influence trade reform? A number of these questions are taken up in more detail in the case studies.

Selection of Fund Arrangements for Review

The review covers all Fund arrangements of two years or more in length that started after January 1, 1990 and that ended by June 30, 1996. Arrangements of less than two years duration are excluded since these typically focus on financial stabilization and would be expected to have less emphasis on structural policies, including trade policy reforms. The cutoff point of mid-1996 was selected to ensure sufficient time had elapsed since the conclusion of the arrangement to permit a proper assessment of performance under the Fund-supported program. On this basis, 30 arrangements supporting 28 programs for 27 countries are reviewed. These include arrangements under the EFF, SAF, and ESAF,[57] as well as two RAPs, and four Stand-By Arrangements.

Country Case Studies

Six countries were selected for detailed case studies to complement the review of trade reform in the context of 28 Fund-supported programs. The case studies cover the 1990–96 period, with earlier periods covered if they relate directly to trade reform in 1990–96, and

[57]The ESAF arrangements with Burundi and Rwanda, both of which began in 1991, are excluded.

consider the following questions. In cases where the Fund-supported programs were not very ambitious, did Fund staff initially propose a more ambitious trade reform in the program negotiations? If trade reform went off track, what factors may have been responsible? In particular, did fiscal constraints, balance of payments problems, or obligations to regional groupings, affect trade reform? What characteristics did successful trade reformers possess that were absent in less successful reformers (e.g., a well-developed tax system)?

Based on results of the reviews of 28 Fund-supported programs, countries were classified into four broad categories: (1) liberalizers where the program included reasonable trade policy conditionality; (2) liberalizers where the program did not include reasonable trade policy conditionality; (3) nonliberalizers where the program included reasonable trade policy conditionality; and (4) nonliberalizers where the program did not include reasonable trade policy conditionality.

Countries with good information on the nature of their trade regime were selected with a view to covering three of the four broad categories (category 2 is of little relevance for the evaluation of Fund programs). The final selection of countries (Bangladesh, Egypt, Hungary, Sri Lanka, Zambia, and Zimbabwe) also took account of a second set of desirable subcriteria:

- nature of conditionality for monitoring trade reform implementation in the program;
- membership in regional trading arrangements that may have influenced the pace of trade reform;
- fiscal or balance of payments constraints; and
- inclusion of countries from different regions of the world.

Overall Trade Restrictiveness Classification Scheme

Table 12 illustrates the assignment of tariff and NTB categories on the 10-point scale. The assignment places more weight on restrictiveness of NTBs, which are inherently less transparent and more distortionary than tariffs.

The restrictiveness of the import tariff regime depends on many factors, including the minimum and maximum tariff rates, the number of bands, the allocation of individual items to the bands, existence of "exceptional" rates that lie outside the basic tariff structure, any other duties and charges (such as differential rates of excise or VAT taxes on imports, import surcharges, and statistical fees), and the extent of customs duty exemptions. The amount of information available on the tariff regime varies considerably among the countries. In many, there was enough information to compute an average tariff rate but insufficient information to assess the degree of tariff dispersion or the prevalence of discretionary customs duty exemptions (as opposed to statutory zero customs duty rates). In view of these limitations, the study adopted a pragmatic approach and used the average import tariff rate as a basis for classifying the tariff regime.[58]

Table 12. Classification Scheme for Overall Trade Restrictiveness

	Nontariff Barriers		
	Open	Moderate	Restrictive
Tariffs			
Open	1	4	7
Relatively open	2	5	8
Moderate	3	6	9
Relatively restrictive	4	7	10
Restrictive	5	8	10

Source: IMF staff estimates.

The five-category ranking of average import tariffs, based on the average tariff rates of Fund member countries, is specified in Table 13.

Broadly equal numbers of Fund members fell into each of these ranges based on the latest available information on average import tariff rates. Alternative ranges were considered in connection with the results of the review.

Countries employ a wide variety of restrictions on imports and exports other than tariffs, including import/export quotas, restrictive licensing, bans, state trading/monopolies, restrictive foreign exchange allocation, and multiple exchange rates. Such measures in effect provide indirect subsidies to import-competing domestic producers in a nontransparent manner. Information on the presence of NTBs and their restrictiveness (as measured for instance by ad valorem equivalents)[59]

[58]The preferred approach was to use, where possible, an unweighted average based on statutory tariff rates and including any other duties and charges applicable to imports. An average of statutory tariff rates is preferable to an average based on customs duties collected since the latter reflect (often extensive) exemptions. An unweighted average is preferable to a trade-weighted average since items with high tariffs would likely have small trade weights. Other duties and charges should be included because they have the same restrictive effects as tariffs.

[59]The ad valorem equivalent of an import quota is the rate of ad valorem tariff that would yield the same import quantity as the quota. There are many circumstances in which import quotas and import tariffs are not equivalent, including where market structures are imperfectly competitive or where trading partners may retaliate against increases in tariffs or quotas; see Bhagwati and Srinivasan (1983) for further discussion and references. Notwithstanding these well-known theoretical difficulties, price equivalents of NTBs are often computed by comparing domestic with world market prices. Quantification of the price equivalent of an export restriction is often accomplished in a similar manner.

Table 13. Classification Scheme for Tariff Restrictiveness

Restrictiveness	Average Tariff Range (t)
Open	$0 \le t < 10$ percent
Relatively open	$10 \le t < 15$ percent
Moderate	$15 \le t < 20$ percent
Relatively restrictive	$20 \le t < 25$ percent
Restrictive	25 percent or over

Source: IMF staff estimates.

may be limited;[60] the review of previous studies on trade reform in developing countries below shows that others have faced similar difficulties. In view of this, Table 14 shows the three ranges of NTBs[61] that have been used in this study.

While more trade variables (such as tariff dispersion or customs duty exemptions) could in principle be included in the overall index of trade restrictiveness, by adding dimensions to the 15-cell matrix, data difficulties and added complexity strongly support the approach of omitting these factors from the overall index. In principle, it would also be preferable to assess the effects of trade restrictions on prices and resource allocation, but this is very difficult and time-consuming even for industrial countries; it is not feasible for the program countries analyzed in this review. The review of previous studies below illustrates these points.

Table 14. Classification Scheme for NTB Restrictiveness

NTB Regime	Classification Criteria
Open	NTBs are either absent or minor. Less than 1 percent of production or trade is subject to NTBs.
Moderate	NTBs are significant, covering at least one important sector of the economy (e.g., agriculture or textiles) but not pervasive (e.g., all consumer goods). Between 1 percent and 25 percent of production or trade is subject to NTBs.
Restrictive	Many sectors or entire stages of production (e.g., all consumer goods) are covered by NTBs. More than 25 percent of production or trade is subject to NTBs.

Source: IMF staff estimates.

Comparison with Approaches in Previous Studies

A number of previous studies have attempted to quantify the extent of trade reform in developing countries. Some have not attempted to form an overall index of trade restrictiveness (Dean, Desai, and Riedel, 1994); others have developed simple indicators of openness (Kirmani and others, 1994b; Papageorgiou, Michaely, and Choksi, 1991; and Sachs and Warner, 1995); while others have formed quantitative measures that summarize the overall stance of the trade and exchange regime based on multiyear research projects (Balassa, 1971; Bhagwati, 1978; and Krueger, 1978). This section examines these previous efforts in relation to the methodology used in the present study to assess the ambitiousness and implementation of trade reform in Fund-supported programs.

Balassa

Bela Balassa (1971) led a research project on the structure of protection in six developing countries (Brazil, Chile, Mexico, West Malaysia, Pakistan, and the Philippines) and, for comparison, one developed country (Norway). The study analyzes the pattern of trade protection in these countries and its implications for resource allocation, exports, and economic growth.

Measures of trade protection were developed, known as effective rates of protection, that aimed to assess how trade protection affected production incentives for different industrial activities:

- Effective rates of protection took account of both nominal rates of protection for imported intermediate inputs and the nominal protection afforded to the final products.
- If import QRs were binding rather than import tariffs, then the differences between domestic and world prices were often used, as measures of the price equivalents of the QRs, to compute effective rates of protection.

Notwithstanding the well-known theoretical limitations of effective protection measures as indicators of resource misallocation, as noted by Bhagwati and Srinivasan (1973), the study makes clear that the calculation of effective rates protection measures require very substantial amounts of information and analysis.

[60] Trade or production coverage of NTBs measures the presence of NTBs but does not fully capture their restrictiveness.

[61] NTBs include quantitative restrictions, state trade monopolies, restrictive foreign exchange practices that affect the trade regime (e.g., a surrender requirement at a nonmarket exchange rate), quality controls and customs procedures that act as trade restrictions. This definition of NTBs is broader than used in the ESAF review (Bredenkamp and others, 1998) and in an earlier Fund study (Kirmani and others, 1994b).

Bhagwati and Krueger

Jagdish Bhagwati (1978) and Anne Krueger (1978) led a study of liberalization of trade and exchange controls. Extensive case studies were prepared for each of the following ten countries: Brazil, Chile, Colombia, Egypt, Ghana, India, Israel, the Philippines, South Korea, and Turkey.

The study analyzes the balance of payments effects of exchange rate devaluation for developing countries with complex exchange control regimes (including trade and exchange restrictions). It decomposes the benefits of moving to a more liberal trade and exchange system following a nominal devaluation into three parts:

- avoidance of static costs of QR regimes due to inefficiencies in licensing and resource misallocation;
- higher growth stemming from increased exports under a more realistic exchange rate; and
- higher growth stemming from improved resource allocation due to reduced antiexport bias of the trade and exchange regime.

To quantify these benefits, detailed information was required on the nature of the trade and exchange regime. For instance, effective exchange rates for exports and imports were calculated to evaluate the extent of antiexport bias; these involved adjusting exchange rates for import tariffs, import surcharges, differences in domestic and foreign prices, and export subsidies.

The study led by Bhagwati and Krueger illustrates the extent of information and analysis required to calculate measures that summarize the effects of the trade and exchange regime on resource allocation and economic growth. The present study focuses on trade liberalization and generally excludes consideration of the exchange regime, except where exchange restrictions clearly act as binding trade restrictions.

Papageorgiou, Michaely, and Choksi

Papageorgiou, Michaely, and Choksi (1991) analyze trade liberalization in 19 countries during 36 trade reform episodes. They consider a wide range of issues, including the extent of trade liberalization as measured by movement along an index that evaluated intervention in the trade regime. The index ranges from 1 to 20, with 1 being the highest possible degree of intervention and 20 being the most "neutral":

- A completely neutral trade regime would prevail if there were no government interference in the trade regime. A value was assigned for each year to track progress toward neutrality over time;
- Authors developed the indices for individual countries based on sets of quantitative or qualitative information that were judged relevant to moving the economy closer toward full neutrality;[62]
- It was not possible to use a common methodology and therefore the indices are not comparable across countries;
- The indices are not intended to provide quantitative measurements.

The present study, in contrast, uses a common methodology for constructing indices of overall trade restrictiveness in each country.

Dean, Desai, and Riedel

Dean, Desai, and Riedel (1994) provide a recent quantitative study of trade liberalization in developing countries. It examines, inter alia, changes in tariffs and NTBs between 1985 and 1993 for the following 32 developing countries: Argentina, Bangladesh, Brazil, Cameroon, Chile, China, Colombia, Costa Rica, Côte d'Ivoire, Democratic Republic of Congo, Ghana, India, Indonesia, Kenya, Korea, Madagascar, Malawi, Malaysia, Mali, Mexico, Nigeria, Pakistan, Peru, Philippines, Senegal, South Africa, Sri Lanka, Tanzania, Thailand, Uganda, Venezuela, and Vietnam.

Where available, data are presented for each country on tariff levels, range, and dispersion, and coverage of quantitative trade restrictions. These measures are used separately to assess progress in trade liberalization, including whether there has simply been a shift in the type of trade protection (e.g., tariffs were used to replace QRs) or whether the level of protection has actually declined. There is, however, no attempt to form an overall measure of trade restrictiveness.

Kirmani and Others

The method of classifying the overall restrictiveness of the trade regime in the present study is similar but more detailed than that employed in the study of trade reforms in Fund-supported programs by Kirmani and others (1994b):

- Tariff regimes are classified based on the average statutory tariff (including other duties and charges), with rates of 10 percent or below classified as relatively open, 10–25 percent as moderate, and above 25 percent as restrictive. The earlier study did not incorporate tariff dispersion or exemptions into the classification of trade regimes due to measurement difficulties;

[62]Information used to construct these indices often included nominal and effective rates of protection, the prevalence and degree of restrictiveness of QRs, the degree of antiexport bias, the extent of divergence of the exchange rate from its equilibrium level, the structure of imports (especially the share of final consumer goods in total imports), subjective evaluations of the degree of friction in the administrative machinery, and so on.

- The restrictiveness of import/export QRs is also classified into three categories based on the proportion of tariff lines subject to QRs as well as the intensity of the QRs, in a manner broadly similar to that used in the present study.

The separate classifications of the tariff and QR regimes are combined into the matrix shown in Table 15:

The classification into only three categories of overall trade restrictiveness provides limited scope to distinguish between the initial position of countries' trade regimes, or to capture movements as trade reform measures are implemented. The more detailed ten-point classification used here provides greater scope to capture changes in overall trade restrictiveness due to trade reform implementation.

Another important difference is that the 1994 study compared, inter alia, the overall restrictiveness of the trade regime for program countries between the end of 1990 and the end of 1993. It did not link any changes in overall restrictiveness to the policy content of the Fund-supported program or its implementation. The present study evaluates the restrictiveness of trade regimes at the outset of the program period for each arrangement, assesses how far the specific trade reform measures included in the Fund-supported program would have moved the trade regime along the ten-point scale if they had been fully implemented, and evaluates restrictiveness of the trade regime at the end of the program period. This methodology examines the trade content of Fund programs, how ambitious they were, and their actual implementation.

Sachs and Warner

Sachs and Warner (1995) consider the relationship between trade openness and economic performance, including notably economic growth. Of concern in the present context is the measure of openness used in the study. A country is judged to be closed if it has at least one of the following characteristics:

- NTBs cover at least 40 percent of trade;
- average import tariffs are at least 40 percent;
- the black market exchange rate is depreciated by at least 20 percent relative to the official exchange rate, on average, during the 1970s or 1980s;
- a socialist economic system (as defined by Kornai (1992)); or
- a state monopoly on major exports.[63]

The study defines an open economy as one in which none of the above five conditions apply. Data on tariffs and NTBs for 1985–88 (taken from Barro and Lee, 1994) who rely mostly on data from the United Nations Committee on Trade and Development (UNCTAD) were used to construct the measures of openness, along with an independent literature review to judge the timing of shifts from a closed to an open trade regime.

[63]A country was judged to have had extreme distortions resulting from an export marketing board based on results from a World Bank study, Husain and Faruquee (1994), which covers only African countries.

Table 15. Overall Classification Scheme Used in the Study by Kirmani and Others

	Quantitative Restrictions		
	Relatively open	Moderate	Restrictive
Tariffs			
Relatively open	Open	Moderate	Restrictive
Moderate	Moderate	Moderate	Restrictive
Restrictive	Restrictive	Restrictive	Restrictive

Source: Kirmani and others (1994b).

Sachs and Warner acknowledge that the chosen criteria would benefit from further refinement, for the following reasons:

- the threshold levels are arbitrary (e.g., a black market premium of at least 20 percent);
- nominal rather than effective rates of protection are used;
- the effect of export subsidies in offsetting the anti-export bias of import protection is not considered; and
- quantification of the effects of NTBs is inherently difficult (the study relies mostly on measures of NTBs used by UNCTAD).

Comparison of the Index with Other Indices

Based on this review of the main studies of trade liberalization in developing countries, the following points can be made regarding the usefulness of the index of overall trade restrictiveness used here in comparison with other indices developed in previous studies. First, the index is more detailed than the binary openness indicator developed in Sachs and Warner (1995). It provides ten overall classifications, in contrast to the three overall ratings distinguished in Kirmani and others (1994b), as well as separate ratings for tariffs and NTBs. Second, the index provides a synthesis of tariff and NTB data that is useful for making policy judgments, compared with that used by Dean, Desai, and Riedel (1994), which tabulates tariff and NTB measures but provides no overall ratings. Third, the index provides a reasonable basis for cross-country comparisons owing to the considerable efforts to develop a common analytical framework, in contrast to the 20-point scales of Papageorgiou, Michaely, and Choksi (1991) that were decidedly not comparable across countries. Fourth, although the index is perhaps not as detailed and precise as the effective rates of protection in Balassa (1971) or the effective exchange rates in Bhagwati (1978) and Krueger (1978), construction of such measures is a massive undertaking for each country case considered. This comparison suggests that the index used here is preferable to those feasible alternatives developed in previous studies.

Appendix II
Summary of the Detailed Case Studies

The findings of the six country case studies that examine trade reform in Bangladesh, Egypt, Hungary, Sri Lanka, Zambia, and Zimbabwe during 1990–96 are summarized below.

Bangladesh

During the period 1990–96, Bangladesh had one Fund arrangement, followed by a program monitored under enhanced surveillance. The ESAF arrangement covered in the review was approved in August 1990 and covered the period through June 1993, and enhanced surveillance was in place during 1993–94.

Notwithstanding a SAF arrangement in 1986/87–1988/89, Bangladesh's trade regime was highly restrictive at the outset of the ESAF arrangement. The unweighted average tariff was estimated at around 89 percent, the maximum rate was over 500 percent, and there were 24 tariff bands. In addition, a development surcharge of 8 percent applied to all imports. Import NTBs were extensive, with 315 tariff line items (or about 25 percent of the total) subject to some form of quantitative restriction. Export NTBs included export restrictions or outright bans on about 20 items, including rice.

Significant progress was achieved in reducing the restrictiveness of Bangladesh's trade system during the ESAF arrangement period, yet it remained restrictive. The unweighted average tariff declined to an estimated 59 percent, the maximum tariff rate fell to 100 percent, the number of tariff bands was reduced to 15, and the development surcharge was eliminated. Also, the number of tariff line items subject to import NTBs was reduced to 93 (or about 7 percent of the total). Jute export subsidies and the minimum export price for jute products were eliminated, but raw jute exports were still subject to an export price check and, more important, export restrictions or outright bans remained. Thus, the overall restrictiveness of Bangladesh's trade regime fell from a rating of 10 in 1990 to 8 in 1993 (Table 16).

Subsequently, considerable further progress was achieved in tariff reduction in the context of the enhanced surveillance program in 1993/94 and of the World Bank Industrial Sector Adjustment Credit (ISAC II). The maximum tariff rate was reduced to 45 percent by 1996 and customs duties on various capital goods, raw materials, and inputs for agriculture and selected industries were either eliminated or reduced. As a result, the unweighted average tariff declined to about 22 percent by 1996/97 and the number of tariff bands fell to 7. However, the number of tariff line items subject to import NTBs rose to 110 (or about 9 percent of the total). Export restrictions or outright bans remained. As a result, the overall restrictiveness of Bangladesh's trade system declined to a rating of 7 by 1996.

Targets and Implementation Under the Fund Program and Trade Reform in Nonprogram Years

The ESAF arrangement sought to rationalize the tariff structure by reducing the maximum rate (except for some luxury goods) and the number of bands, and to phase out import NTBs. In addition, bans and restrictions on imports were to be reduced substantially, except for a small number of "sensitive" items. Virtually all import restrictions on items required by exporters were to be removed and the existing duty drawback system for exports was to be strengthened. The elimination of export subsidies was envisaged, except for jute exports; the latter were to be phased out on a more gradual basis. Trade reform targets, most of which were monitored via prior actions, were met.

Subsequently, there was some further liberalization of Bangladesh's trade regime in the context of the enhanced surveillance program and the World Bank ISAC II. The latter provided for, inter alia, removal of import controls, rationalization of the tariff structure, implementation of trade neutral taxes, including the VAT, and a strengthening of customs administration. As noted above, tariffs were reduced, but import NTBs rose.

Factors Affecting Design and Implementation of Trade Reform in Fund Program

A major factor affecting the pace of trade reform was the authorities' concern about the negative impact of trade liberalization on the balance of payments and fiscal positions (customs duties accounted for more than 30 percent of tax revenue). Equally important, the negotiations on trade reform under the ISAC II with

Table 16. Bangladesh: Restrictiveness of Trade Regime

	1990	1991	1992	1993	1994	1995	1996
Actual	10	10	8	8	7	7	7
Program	n.a.	10	8	8	n.a.	n.a.	n.a.

Source: IMF staff estimates.
Scale: 1 (least restrictive) to 10 (most restrictive). n.a. denotes not applicable.

the World Bank were protracted and affected the quality of medium-term trade reform targets in the ESAF program, which were to be based on the outcome of these negotiations. Also, the importance of the textile industry hampered removal of NTBs protecting this sector. Prior actions were used to monitor the implementation of trade reform under the ESAF arrangement to highlight the importance of trade reform.

In general, other factors such as membership in RTAs and commitments to the GATT/WTO appear not to have affected the pace of trade reform. Bangladesh's tariff bindings under the Uruguay Round were well above the applied rates and would not have entailed further liberalization of its trade regime. The overall macroeconomic framework remained on track throughout, with all financial and structural performance criteria observed on a timely basis.

Conclusion

While considerable trade liberalization took place, especially on the import tariff structure, Bangladesh's trade system remained relatively restrictive at the end of 1996. The critical nature of trade reform was reflected in the use of prior actions in the ESAF arrangement and most trade reform targets were met in a timely manner. A key factor hindering trade reform, however, was the authorities' concern about the potentially negative effect of trade reform on the fiscal and balance of payments positions. Protracted negotiations between the authorities and Bank staff resulted in a weak and less focused specification of medium-term trade reform targets under the ESAF arrangement.

Bangladesh's experience points to the need to implement trade reform in the context of a comprehensive macroeconomic adjustment program to, inter alia, reduce pressures on the fiscal and external positions. In this regard, the lack of well-specified, medium-term trade reform targets and supporting intermediate steps may have impeded trade reform. Given Bangladesh's heavy reliance on trade taxes, early adoption of a trade-neutral tax structure, including the VAT, might have helped trade reform to proceed without unduly affecting the fiscal position. It also points to the ability of an important industrial sector to resist early dismantling of import barriers that protect it.

Egypt

During the period 1990–96, Egypt had three Fund arrangements. Besides the May 1991 Stand-By Arrangement covered in the review, which covered the period through June 1993, a successor three-year EFF arrangement was approved in September 1993. A two-year Stand-By Arrangement was approved in October 1996.

Egypt had a restrictive trade system in 1990, ranked 10 on the scale of trade restrictiveness (Table 17). The general tariff schedule ranged from zero to 120 percent, but there were exceptions with substantially higher rates applied to a few "luxury" and other goods that included cosmetics, automobiles, alcohol, and tobacco. The unweighted average tariff was estimated at about 35 percent in 1990. Although Egypt's import licensing scheme was abolished in 1986, import bans covered about one-third of tradable goods output in late 1990. Also, some 56 tariff line items required import prior approvals. There were export taxes on nine tariff line items, but some of these were not binding as the same products were covered by bans. In late 1990, export prior approvals and export bans covered, respectively, 8 percent and 7 percent of tradable goods output. In addition, a further 17 tariff line items—covering about 1 percent of tradable goods output—were subject to export quotas.

Despite progress with trade liberalization in 1990–96, Egypt's trade system remained restrictive at the end of the period and ranked 8 on the scale of trade restrictiveness at the end of 1996.[64] The general tariff schedule ranged from zero to 55 percent. Substantially higher tariff rates applied to alcohol, tobacco, and automobiles, and import surcharges of 2 percent or 4 percent applied to all imports. The unweighted average tariff was estimated at above 25 percent. While import bans were substantially reduced during the Stand-By Arrangement of 1991–93,[65] there is evi-

[64]Additional trade liberalization has been implemented so far in 1997 with the maximum tariff rate (and other intermediate rates) reduced by 5 percentage points. Further liberalization is planned for 1998.

[65]There are import bans on textiles and garments estimated to cover less than 5 percent of tradable goods output. As part of the Uruguay Round agreement, Egypt has agreed to eliminate the import ban on textiles by January 1, 1998 and on clothing by January 1, 2001. An import ban on poultry was eliminated in July 1997.

Table 17. Egypt: Restrictiveness of Trade Regime

	1990	1991	1992	1993	1994	1995	1996
Actual	10	10	8	8	8	8	8
Program[1]	n.a.	10	8	8	5	4[2]	8[3]

Source: IMF staff estimates.

Scale: 1 (least restrictive) to 10 (most restrictive). n.a. denotes not applicable.

[1]Under the Stand-By Arrangement of 1996–98, the restrictiveness of Egypt's trade regime is expected to decline to a rating of 4 by mid-1998.

[2]This rating refers to the target under the 1993 Extended Fund Facility (EFF) for the end of 1995.

[3]This rating refers to the target under the 1996 Stand-By Arrangement for the end of 1996.

dence that some have been replaced by restrictive quality controls. In addition, there are cumbersome customs procedures. All export taxes were eliminated in late 1992, and the only remaining export NTB is a ban on exports of raw hides, which is scheduled to be removed in 1998.

Targets and Implementation Under Fund Programs

The program for the 1991 Stand-By Arrangement aimed to reduce the trade regime's restrictiveness by 2 points. The range of general tariff rates was to be reduced to 10–80 percent by June 1992, and thereafter tariff reform was expected to reduce further dispersion and the average rate, as well as to eliminate exceptions to the general tariff structure and to reduce preferences. On import NTBs, import bans were scheduled to be reduced significantly by June 1992, and import prior approvals were to be phased out. Export bans would be reduced, export quotas increased, and export prior approvals eliminated.

Most trade reform measures were implemented as envisaged in the early part of the program. Restoration of customs duty rates to their early-1989 levels (within the new general tariff schedule) was a prior action and an integral part of the fiscal revenue package, and increased the average tariff to 42 percent. For the first review, trade reform was implemented as envisaged. The reduction and elimination of NTBs was greater than programmed. The second stage of trade reform, linked to the World Bank Structural Adjustment Loan (SAL), was delayed. The general maximum tariff was reduced with a delay, while the minimum rate remained unchanged.[66] The program reduced tariff dispersion, but the unweighted average tariff remained high and was estimated at 34 percent at the end of the program. Substantial progress was made in removing both import and export NTBs, but the number of products subject to restrictive quality controls increased.

The 1993 EFF program aimed at substantial trade liberalization, that is, a movement of 4 points on the scale of trade restrictiveness. The maximum general tariff rate was to be reduced from 80 percent to 70 percent by December 1993 with a corresponding reduction in all tariff rates above 30 percent. Thereafter, tariff reform was expected to reduce dispersion and the average rate by lowering, in two stages, the maximum general tariff to 50 percent by December 1995 with corresponding reductions in tariff rates above 30 percent. Tariff rates at 30 percent or below were to remain largely unaffected, but tariffs on some capital goods were to be reduced to 5 or 10 percent by December 1995. All but one of the exceptions to the general tariff structure were to be eliminated by June 1994.

On import NTBs, all import bans were eliminated in June 1993, except on textiles, garments, and poultry. The import ban on poultry was to be eliminated by June 1994, and the other bans were to be addressed by the ongoing Uruguay Round negotiations. In addition, the authorities were committed to implement GATT rules for quality control standards by June 1994. Remaining export NTBs were to be eliminated by June 1995.

Reflecting the importance accorded to trade reform, the program relied heavily on prior actions to monitor trade policy implementation. They included the public announcement of Egypt's medium-term trade reform plans. However, the structural reform component of the program was not implemented as envisaged; limited trade liberalization was accomplished; and the restrictiveness of Egypt's trade system did not change substantially. Although the maximum tariff, tariffs on capital goods, and tariff dispersion were reduced, the unweighted average tariff remained high, estimated at 32 percent at the end of the program period. Also, import surcharges at the rates of 2 percent and 5 percent were introduced for fiscal revenue reasons in April 1994. No progress was made in eliminating the restrictive features of quality controls on imports, and, therefore, NTBs did not change significantly. Tariff reform was postponed on the grounds that it would have imposed an "unacceptable burden" on lower-income groups.

The 1996 Stand-By Arrangement program aims at a substantial reduction in the restrictiveness of Egypt's trade system, amounting to a movement of 4 points on the scale mainly through the elimination of the re-

[66]The increase of the minimum tariff would have breached some of Egypt's GATT bindings, and therefore not all of this increase took place.

maining import NTBs and further tariff reductions. As in the EFF, the importance of the trade reform was signaled via prior actions. These prior actions were significant and included the public reaffirmation of the government's commitment to medium-term trade liberalization and faster integration in the world economy, as well as significant tariff reductions in the general maximum rate (to 55 percent) and rates above 30 percent.[67] Thereafter, the general maximum tariff rate is expected to be reduced in two stages to 40 percent by July 1998 (with tariffs between 30–50 percent to be reduced to 30 percent).[68] In addition, the import surcharge will be reduced and unified at 1 percent by July 1998.[69] Tariffs on automobiles were initially cut in October 1996 and are to be reduced over the next five years, but the other exceptions to the general tariff structure (alcohol and tobacco) are not scheduled to be eliminated during the program period. The import ban on poultry was eliminated in July 1997 and replaced with an 80 percent tariff. Egypt's system of mandatory quality controls on imports is being reviewed and will be modified in the second half of 1997 to eliminate its restrictive features.

Factors Affecting Design and Implementation of Trade Reform in Fund Programs

The 1991 Stand-By Arrangement. Most of the trade liberalization measures in the program were designed under the auspices of the World Bank SAL. Fund staff noted on several occasions that a decision by the Bank to proceed with a SAL would be required to proceed with a Stand-By Arrangement, but there was little discussion of specific trade measures in the program, except the increase in custom duties for fiscal reasons. However, the balance of payments position was vulnerable and may have affected the design of trade liberalization measures. The second stage of trade reform was delayed because of employment and political economy considerations.

The 1993 EFF. The main trade-related measures in the program were designed in close collaboration with Bank staff and were part of the World Bank Structural Adjustment Monitoring Program. The negotiations over the structural reform measures in the EFF were protracted. The Fund staff favored ambitious trade reform, but the final program had a more gradual pace. In negotiations, the authorities were concerned that faster trade liberalization could worsen unemployment, although the need for liberalization in the longer term was recognized. Implementation was influenced by employment and political concerns.

The 1996 Stand-By Arrangement. Program negotiations were again protracted and centered on structural reforms. Although the main trade reform measures were designed based on earlier Fund-Bank work on trade liberalization, the Bank was not directly involved. In the negotiations, the Fund staff's initial position in the area of trade reform was ambitious but the final program had a more gradual pace of trade liberalization. Throughout the negotiations, the authorities advocated a more measured pace of structural reforms, including trade reform, for reasons of political economy. They also expressed concern about the impact of reductions in tariffs and the import surcharge on the fiscal position.

Conclusion

Substantial trade liberalization was implemented by Egypt in the 1990s, with Fund and World Bank assistance, but its trade system remained restrictive at the end of 1996, although further liberalization is proceeding in 1997 and planned for 1998. Egypt's macroeconomic environment improved throughout most of the period. A more gradual approach to trade liberalization was adopted owing to fears that faster reform could have worsened unemployment in the short run and to maintain the domestic political consensus.

Egypt's experience shows that trade reform can be implemented together with fiscal adjustment. It demonstrates the ability to reinject momentum in trade liberalization after a slowdown in these reforms. Also, it points to the need to adopt measures to address possible adverse effects of trade reform on domestic production and employment in the short run.

Hungary

During the period 1990–96, Hungary had four Fund arrangements. The 12-month Stand-By Arrangement approved in March 1990 did not contain trade reform. It was replaced in February 1991 by the EFF covered in the review. A new Stand-By Arrangement was approved in September 1993 but did not contain trade reform; fiscal difficulties contributed to this program going off track in 1994. A two-year Stand-By Arrangement was approved in March 1996.

In 1990, Hungary had a restrictive trade system, ranked 10 on the scale of restrictiveness. The unweighted average tariff rate was about 21 percent (including 5 percent customs fees) with a high dispersion of rates. Tariff exemptions were widespread and, for example, about 40 percent of imports (from CMEA partners) were not subject to customs duties. About three-fourths of imports were subject to NTBs (mostly restrictive licenses), including a quota on consumer

[67]The maximum tariff rate and tariff rates above 50 percent were reduced by 15 percentage points, and tariff rates of 40–50 percent by 10 percentage points.

[68]The first set of tariff reductions was implemented on July 1, 1997.

[69]The higher rate surcharge was reduced from 4 percent to 3 percent on July 1, 1997.

goods imports amounting to $200 million, or the equivalent to 2 percent of imports. Trading monopolies covered products accounting for about 20 percent of imports and 35 percent of exports. There were no export taxes, but all exports were subject to licencing. Export subsidies existed for CMEA trade and for agricultural exports. In addition, foreign exchange restrictions acted as a trade barrier.

Hungary's trade regime was substantially liberalized during 1990–96 and ranked 6 on the scale of restrictiveness by the end of 1996 (Table 18). Most trade liberalization occurred in 1991 in the context of the EFF when the CMEA managed trade system moved to world prices, which resulted in a considerable reduction in NTBs. However, subsequent progress in reducing the remaining import NTBs, which cover 7–10 percent of imports (mostly linked to the consumer goods quota), has been limited. The remaining export licenses concern mostly products subject to restrictions in export markets (an estimated 30–40 percent of exports). The unweighted average tariff rate declined to 18 percent in 1991 (tariff 13 percent, customs fees 5 percent), where it remained until 1994. However, it increased to about 22 percent in 1995 when Hungary introduced an import surcharge of 8 percent, partly offset by a reduction in basic tariffs under its Uruguay Round commitments. In 1996, the unweighted average tariff rate was reduced to 18 percent as the surcharge rate declined to 6 percent, tariff cuts related to the Uruguay Round continued, and customs fees were reduced from 4 percent to 2 percent. A number of other export distortions remained, such as export subsidies for agricultural products. Finally, exchange restrictions were gradually liberalized, notwithstanding some tightening in 1990–92, and the currency became convertible in 1996. The surcharge was removed in mid-1997.

Targets and Implementation Under Fund Programs

Two of the four Fund-supported programs contained trade reform. The 1991 EFF required Hungary to liberalize import licenses, including a shift of the CMEA trade to world prices, and to increase the quota on consumer goods imports. The 1996 Stand-By Arrangement included the phasing out of the import surcharge and a commitment to reduce the number of consumption goods subject to the import quota.

All of the above-mentioned targets were met and sometimes exceeded. The trade reform under the 1991 EFF was implemented despite the fiscal difficulties encountered in the programs, and Hungary reduced the import surcharge ahead of the schedule agreed with the Fund in 1996.

Factors Affecting Design and Implementation of Trade Reform in Fund Programs

External factors affecting trade reform usually emerged in the design stage. Balance of payments concerns may explain the lack of trade reform in the program supported by the 1990 Stand-By Arrangement. The design of the 1991 EFF was influenced positively by the improved current account position, and an acknowledged need for structural reform by the government. Trade reform was closely coordinated with the World Bank. Since 1992, regional trading arrangements may have influenced Hungary's willingness to undertake broader nondiscriminatory trade reform, as trade policy was linked to its free trade agreement with the European Union (EU). The 1993 Stand-By Arrangement did not contain any trade reform. Fund staff had suggested that further trade reform was needed, and the lack of trade reform may have been influenced by the difficult fiscal and balance of payments positions as well as the substantial increase in unemployment in the preceding years. The design of the 1996 Stand-By Arrangement, in which Fund staff had initially proposed more substantial trade reform, may have been influenced by the fragile fiscal situation and protectionist lobbying. The agreed phase-out of the surcharge was more gradual than that proposed by the Fund staff. The desire to protect some local industries and ongoing liberalization in the GATT-WTO context were cited as reasons for not eliminating the remaining NTBs. On trade reform implementation, the government's commitment to liberalization was an important factor, particularly in the early 1990s when Hungary implemented trade reform despite the rest of the program running into difficulties, and at other times when trade liberalization exceeded program targets. Also, as mentioned above, the phasing out of the surcharge in 1996 was implemented faster than was agreed in the program.

Table 18. Hungary: Restrictiveness of Trade Regime

	1990	1991	1992	1993	1994	1995	1996
Actual	10	6	6	6	6	7	6
Program	10	7	7	6	6	n.a.	6

Source: IMF staff estimates.
Scale: 1 (least restrictive) to 10 (most restrictive). n.a. denotes not applicable.

Conclusion

The most important factor promoting trade reform in Hungary may have been the government's commitment to undertake reform. Its desire to dismantle central planning was a major policy objective and influenced liberalization, following the collapse of the CMEA trading system. Subsequently, NTB reduction has been slower and progress with tariff reform mixed. Tariffs were lowered in the context of WTO obligations, but a surcharge was introduced. Hungary's desire to liberalize only in the context of the GATT-WTO and regional agreements may have slowed down the pace of trade reform. For example, the authorities were reluctant to undertake further reductions in the quota on consumer goods imports partly because this could have reduced leverage in international trade negotiations. Fiscal and balance of payments difficulties critically affected overall program implementation and, at times, the pace of trade reform.

Sri Lanka

During the period 1990–96, Sri Lanka had one Fund arrangement. The ESAF was approved in September 1991 and covered the period through July 1995. It continued the structural reforms initiated in the context of the 1988–91 SAF.

Sri Lanka had a moderately restrictive trade system initially, classified as a 7 on the scale of restrictiveness. The average tariff was estimated at 16 percent in 1990, and the maximum rate was 60 percent. In addition, there was a 2½ percent stamp duty on import letters of credit and a markup of 25 percent was applied to the c.i.f. value of imported (but not domestic) goods for the calculation of domestic indirect taxes. There were a number of specific duties that in some cases had ad valorem equivalents in excess of 100 percent. As a result, combined average tariff protection was probably 20–25 percent at the outset of the ESAF. NTBs were significant but not pervasive. A significant number of items were subject to import licensing and to import monopolies and several items were subject to export licensing. Export taxes applied principally to Sri Lanka's traditional exports of tea, rubber, and coconut products.

Substantial liberalization of the trade regime was achieved in 1990–96 moving Sri Lanka to a rating of 2 on the scale of restrictiveness (Table 19). By the end of the ESAF in 1995, Sri Lanka had an average tariff estimated at 8 percent. The maximum rate was reduced to 35 percent. However, the markup of 25 percent applied to the c.i.f. value of imported (but not domestic) goods in the calculation of domestic indirect taxes probably pushed overall average tariff protection to above 10 percent. Tariff reform lost momentum after the end of the program, and a planned shift to a two-band tariff system, with a maximum rate of 25 percent, was delayed in part for fiscal reasons. Import NTBs were largely removed during the program, and in 1996, import licensing was further scaled back. By the end of the program period, export licensing was restricted to items justified for environmental or cultural reasons only. Export taxes had been largely eliminated in the course of the program.

Targets and Implementation Under the Fund Program

The ESAF sought to reduce average tariffs while reducing dispersion and the maximum rate from 50 percent to 35 percent. Also, it sought to eliminate import and export NTBs as well as export taxes. The program had extensive conditionality on trade reform to signal its importance. The first stage of Sri Lanka's trade reform, including a reduction in the maximum rate and in the number of tariff bands, was monitored by a structural performance criterion in the first annual arrangement. The second stage of trade reform was monitored by a structural benchmark in the second annual arrangement, and the third stage, covering the elimination of most import and export licensing requirements, was a prior action for the third (and final) annual arrangement.

Trade reform was generally implemented as envisaged, aside from some minor deviations and delays. Some tariff reform measures planned for April and June 1993 were implemented in November 1993 as part of the 1994 budget. A more substantial delay was the reduction in the maximum tariff rate to 35 percent, which did not take place until early 1995. However, the trade regime at the end of the program was essentially that envisaged in the program.

Factors Affecting Design and Implementation of Trade Reform in Fund Program

Sri Lanka's trade reform was largely implemented as initially planned, which reflected, inter alia, the commitment of the authorities. Toward the end of the ESAF, negotiations became more protracted. Trade reform, however, does not seem generally to have been a significant factor in delaying the negotiations.

Fiscal policy was probably an important factor influencing the design, negotiation, and implementation of trade reform. The program ultimately went off track for fiscal reasons in 1994. It seems unlikely that trade reform in the program, which included reductions in tariffs and export taxes, was considered in isolation given Sri Lanka's dependence on trade taxes and its large fiscal deficits. The World Bank was involved by providing technical assistance on trade reform.

Balance of payments considerations and membership in RTAs do not appear to have affected the pace of trade reform. The reason for this may be related to

Table 19. Sri Lanka: Restrictiveness of Trade Regime

	1990	1991	1992	1993	1994	1995	1996
Actual	7	7	6	2	2	2	2
Program	n.a.	n.a.	6	2	2	2	n.a.

Source: IMF staff estimates.
Scale: 1 (least restrictive) to 10 (most restrictive). n.a. denotes not applicable.

Sri Lanka's access to highly concessional external financing, including grants. Although Sri Lanka is a member of the South Asian Preferential Trading Arrangement, the preferences extended by (and to) Sri Lanka under this RTA have been limited so far.[70]

It is not clear whether other factors were behind the slippages in trade reform in 1994. The elections may have affected the pace of trade reform as election-related spending led to fiscal pressures and political considerations in an election year promoting protectionist interests.

Conclusion

Sri Lanka had begun to liberalize its trade regime in 1977. An important factor in its relative success at liberalization in the 1990s was the commitment of the successive governments (of both major parties) to trade reform. Although at times fiscal policy may have affected the pace of trade reform, the serious fiscal deficits in Sri Lanka have not stopped trade reform, including the implementation of some revenue-reducing elements of trade reform.

Zambia

During the 1990–96 period, Zambia had three Fund-supported programs. The RAP of July 1992 followed the RAP of 1991, which went off track. The 1992 RAP was negotiated against the background of a severe shortfall in food supplies and of worsened fiscal and balance of payments positions. Following the accumulation of rights and the repayment of Zambia's arrears to the Fund, the SAF-ESAF–supported program came into effect in December 1995.

Zambia started the period with a moderately restrictive trade regime that ranked 7 on the scale of restrictiveness (Table 20). In late 1990, as part of a World Bank–supported effort, the maximum tariff rate was gradually reduced to 50 percent (from 100 percent), while the minimum rate was increased to 15 percent (from zero). Tariff protection, however, was also affected by the sales tax on imports, as some imports were exempted from the sales tax while other imports were subject to a de facto higher sales tax rate. In addition, a licensing levy of 5 percent applied to imports subject to licensing. Zambia granted numerous tariff exemptions under the Investment Code as well as for imports by the government, the state mining company, and numerous (privatized) companies and charitable institutions. Finally, mining exports were taxed at 20 percent, although exemptions were allowed, and the state mining company was exempted, as it was already paying the mineral resources levy.

Zambia implemented an impressive trade reform program in 1990–96 and currently has one of the more liberal trade regimes in Africa, ranking 3 on the scale of restrictiveness. Zambia's participation in the CBI trade and investment initiative has been an important factor in furthering reform. The 1996 budget included further tariff reform measures significantly ahead of schedule according to Zambia's commitments under the CBI and Common Market for Eastern and Southern Africa (COMESA). As a result, the maximum tariff rate was reduced to 25 percent and the (general) minimum rate to 5 percent in February 1996, although some inputs and machinery continue to be rated zero. There are now only four tariff bands (zero, 5, 15, and 25 percent) and the unweighted average tariff rate is estimated at 13.6 percent. The import declaration fee of 5 percent, however, was not abolished at the end of 1996 as envisaged, but the authorities have indicated their intention to remove this surcharge at the end of 1997. Zambia's trade regime is essentially free of import and export NTBs.

Targets and Implementation Under Fund Programs and in Nonprogram Years

The Fund programs sought to move Zambia by 4 points on the scale of trade restrictiveness during the period. The 1992 RAP program was mainly concerned with liberalizing Zambia's restrictive exchange regime that severely restricted trade. There was a clear understanding that as Zambia had made considerable progress with trade reform, recurring fiscal slippages imposed limits on the tariff reform that could be pur-

[70]Sri Lanka extends concessions on 31 tariff lines only and the margin of preference ranges between 10 percent and 20 percent of the general tariff rate. Concessions to Sri Lanka by other members are similarly minor.

Table 20. Zambia: Restrictiveness of Trade Regime

	1990	1991	1992	1993	1994	1995	1996
Actual	7	7	7	4	4	4	3
Program	n.a.	n.a.	n.a.	4	4	4	4

Source: IMF staff estimates.
Scale: 1 (least restrictive) to 10 (most restrictive). n.a. denotes not applicable.

sued, and that the World Bank would take the lead. Toward the end of the program, Zambia's obligations to the CBI were the basis for future reforms. The only trade policy target monitored by binding conditionality was the abolition of the import licensing requirement in June 1993, which was observed on a timely basis. Fund programs also envisaged introduction of a VAT, achieved in 1995.

During the 1992 RAP, the import licensing fee equal to 10 percent was abolished in January 1993, and in June 1993 all licensing requirements were also removed. In 1994, the maximum tariff was reduced to 40 percent. In October 1995, faced with fiscal disequilibria, the government introduced a 5 percent import surcharge. Despite this reversal, in early 1996 Zambia further liberalized its trade regime to conform, ahead of the October 1998 deadline, with its CBI obligations. In general, Zambia implemented most commitments in the programs.

Factors Affecting Design and Implementation of Trade Reform in Fund Programs

The need to address fiscal problems and liberalize the exchange regime was accorded priority over trade issues in the Fund programs. Fund-Bank collaboration in trade reform was effective. There was also an implicit acceptance by the IMF staff of the authorities' commitment to trade reform.

Conclusion

Zambia has succeeded in implementing an impressive trade reform program since the late 1980s. Starting with a very complex and highly restrictive exchange and trade regime, it now has one of the more liberal trade regimes in Africa. This was done in advance of the country's obligations to the CBI and COMESA and generally exceeded the liberalization envisaged under Fund programs. Maximum tariffs were reduced and export restrictions were largely removed. The only setback was the introduction in 1995 of the 5 percent import surcharge.

The authorities' commitment to trade reform has been demonstrated by their actions to liberalize trade ahead of commitments to the Fund and other institutions. Fund-Bank collaboration also appears to have supported trade reform. Zambia's participation in the CBI has promoted trade reform. Recurrent fiscal pressures however, put strains on reform efforts. In 1995, the imposition of a surcharge was a response to redress fiscal slippages.

Zambia started the period with severe external and fiscal imbalances and a highly regulated domestic economy. Initially, Fund programs focused on fiscal consolidation and exchange liberalization to pave the way for the rapid and durable trade liberalization.

Zimbabwe

During the period 1990–96, Zimbabwe had a program supported by closely related Fund arrangements. The EFF and ESAF arrangements covered the period July 1992 to June 1995. It replaced the three-year EFF that had come into effect in January 1992 and was canceled when Zimbabwe became eligible to use ESAF resources. The policy content of the EFF and ESAF was similar to that of the original EFF. The program expired without the scheduled third annual arrangement.

In 1990, Zimbabwe's economy was heavily regulated. The trade regime ranked 10 on the scale of restrictiveness. Tariffs averaged some 20 percent and were supplemented by a 20 percent import surcharge. Thus, average tariff protection, including the surcharge, was some 40 percent. Also, import licensing was used to ration foreign exchange and exporters were required to surrender their export earnings at the (overvalued) official exchange rate. The import and export of many agriculture products were restricted to marketing boards.

Zimbabwe's trade system was somewhat liberalized in 1990–96, owing mainly to the near elimination of its import licensing system. As a result, Zimbabwe moved to a rating of 8 on the scale of trade restrictiveness (Table 21). Notwithstanding the reductions in the import surcharge, tariffs remained high and averaged some 30 percent by the end of the period.

Targets and Implementation Under Fund Programs

The programs aimed at moving Zimbabwe by 4 points to 6 on the scale of trade restrictiveness. The main trade reform measures were liberalizing Zimbabwe's import licensing system as well as eliminat-

Table 21. Zimbabwe: Restrictiveness of Trade Regime

	1990	1991	1992	1993	1994	1995	1996
Actual	10	10	10	8	8	8	8
EFF	n.a.	n.a.	8	8	6	n.a.	n.a.
EFF/ESAF	n.a.	n.a.	n.a.	8	8	6	n.a.

Source: IMF staff estimates.
Scale: 1 (least restrictive) to 10 (most restrictive). n.a. denotes not applicable.

ing the import surcharge. This was to be achieved by expanding the unrestricted Open General Import License (OGIL) system and the Export Retention Scheme (ERS). The products on the OGIL list could be imported by anyone and the list of eligible products was expanded. The ERS allowed exporters to retain a certain percentage of their export receipts, to be used to import eligible products. ERS expansion increased the retention share and expanded the list of eligible products for importation using foreign exchange retained under the ERS. Early in the EFF and ESAF arrangements, with support from IMF staff, the authorities decided to place greater emphasis on ERS expansion as the main vehicle of import liberalization and the envisaged liberalization of import licensing was achieved. Commitments to reduce tariff protection, however, were largely limited to the elimination of the import surcharge, with a reduction from 20 percent to 10 percent by June 1993 and elimination by June 1995.

Implementation of the EFF arrangement was weakened by a number of factors, including severe drought, and therefore the envisaged trade reform was not achieved. During the successor EFF and ESAF arrangements, not all trade reform targets were met. Trade policy commitments monitored by binding conditionality were satisfactorily implemented: the ERS expansion was achieved in a more ambitious form, following the decision to concentrate on the ERS and to discontinue the OGIL. The reduction of the import surcharge to 10 percent was delayed, however, until 1994, and its elimination was not achieved.

Factors Affecting Design and Implementation of Trade Reform in Fund-Supported Programs

Zimbabwe's relatively weak overall economic performance in the 1980s was an important factor influencing economic reform efforts, including trade reform. This could explain why no substantial differences of opinion seem to have emerged during the program design stage. The authorities had charted a course of reform starting in 1990, and IMF and World Bank involvement provided further credibility to the measures. However, the very difficult fiscal situation and the impact of the drought may have influenced the pace of trade liberalization in the design stages. Reform of the foreign exchange and import licensing regime was clearly recognized as a high priority. Tariff reform was accorded a lower priority, and there were some misgivings about tariff reform, given the difficult fiscal situation. Furthermore, with the elimination of import licensing, pressure for import protection through tariffs increased.

Conclusion

The authorities made a good deal of progress liberalizing imports through elimination of the import licensing scheme but were reluctant to move rapidly on trade reform, perhaps because of the impact of the drought, which affected the political economy of trade reform. The main failure in the area of trade reform was the inability to adhere to the schedule of surcharge reduction and elimination. This may have been part of a broader problem related to the overall macroeconomic targets, including fiscal slippages.

Bibliography

Balassa, Bela A., 1971, *The Structure of Protection in Developing Countries* (Baltimore, Maryland: Johns Hopkins Press).

Baldwin, Robert E., 1985, *The Political Economy of U.S. Import Policy* (Cambridge, Massachusetts: MIT Press).

Barro, Robert J., and Jong-Wha Lee, 1994, "Data Set for a Panel of 138 Countries," (unpublished; Cambridge, Massachusetts: Harvard University).

Barro, Robert J., and Xavier Sala-i-Martin, 1995, *Economic Growth* (New York: McGraw-Hill Book Co.).

Bhagwati, Jagdish N., 1978, *Anatomy and Consequences of Exchange Control Regimes* (Cambridge, Massachusetts; New York: Ballinger Publishing Co.).

———, 1982, "Directly Unproductive, Profit-Seeking (DUP) Activities," *Journal of Political Economy,* Vol. 90, No. 5, pp. 988–1002.

Bhagwati, Jagdish N., and T. N. Srinivasan, 1973, "The General Equilibrium Theory of Effective Protection," *Journal of International Economics,* Vol. 3, pp. 259–81.

———, 1983, *Lectures in International Trade* (Cambridge, Massachusetts: MIT Press).

Brecher, Richard A., and Carlos F. Diaz-Alejandro, 1977, "Tariffs, Foreign Capital, and Immiserizing Growth," *Journal of International Economics,* Vol. 7, pp. 317–22.

Bredenkamp, Hugh W., and others, 1998, *The ESAF at Ten Years: Economic Adjustment and Reform in Low Income Countries,* IMF Occasional Paper No. 156. (Washington: International Monetary Fund).

Coe, David T., and Elhanan Helpman, 1993, "International R&D Spillovers," IMF Working Paper 93/84 (Washington: International Monetary Fund).

Dean, Judith M., Seema Desai, and James Riedel, 1994, "Trade Policy Reform in Developing Countries Since 1985: A Review of the Evidence," World Bank Discussion Papers No. 267 (Washington: World Bank).

Dixit, Avinash, 1985, "Tax Policy in Open Economies" in *Handbook of Public Economics,* Vol. 1, ed. by A. J. Auerbach and M. Feldstein (Amsterdam: North-Holland), pp. 313–74.

Faria, Angelo G.A., and M. Zühtü Yücelik, 1995, "The Interrelationship Between Tax Policy and Tax Administration" in *Tax Policy Handbook,* ed. by Parthasarathi Shome (Washington: International Monetary Fund).

Frankel, Jeffrey A., David Romer, and Teresa Cyrus, 1996, "Trade and Growth in East Asian Countries: Cause and Effect?" NBER Working Paper 5732 (Cambridge, Massachusetts: National Bureau of Economic Research).

General Agreement on Tariffs and Trade, 1990, *Trade Policy Review of New Zealand* (Geneva).

———, 1991, *Trade Policy Review of Chile* (Geneva).

Husain, Ishrat, and Rashid Faruquee, eds., 1994, *Adjustment in Africa: Lessons from Country Case Studies* (Washington: World Bank).

International Monetary Fund, 1993, *World Economic Outlook, May 1993: A Survey by the Staff of the International Monetary Fund,* World Economic and Financial Surveys (Washington: International Monetary Fund).

Kirmani, Naheed, and others, 1994a, *Trade Policy Reform in the Countries of the Former Soviet Union,* IMF Economic Review No. 2 (Washington: International Monetary Fund).

———, 1994b, *International Trade Policies: The Uruguay Round and Beyond,* Vol. I, *Principal Issues,* and Vol. II, *Background Papers,* World Economic and Financial Surveys (Washington: International Monetary Fund).

Kornai, Janos, 1992, *The Socialist System: The Political Economy of Communism* (Princeton, New Jersey: Princeton University Press).

Krueger, Anne O., 1974, "The Political Economy of the Rent-Seeking Society," *American Economic Review,* Vol. 64, pp. 291–303.

———,1978, *Liberalization Attempts and Consequences* (Cambridge, Massachusetts: Ballinger Publishing Co.).

———, 1993, *Political Economy of Policy Reform in Developing Countries* (Cambridge, Massachusetts; London, England: MIT Press).

Leidy, Michael P., 1995, "The Political Economy of Trade Policy and the Implications for Trade Policy Reform" (unpublished; Washington: International Monetary Fund).

———, and Ali Ibrahim, 1996, *Recent Trade Policies and an Approach for Further Reform in the Baltics, Russia, and Other Countries of the Former Soviet Union,* IMF Working Paper 96/71 (Washington: International Monetary Fund).

Magee, Stephen P., William A. Brock, and Leslie Young, 1989, *Black Hole Tariffs and Endogenous Policy Theory: Political Economy in General Equilibrium* (Cambridge: Cambridge University Press).

Mussa, Michael, 1986, "The Adjustment Process and the Timing of Trade Liberalization," in *Economic Liberalization in Developing Countries,* ed. by Armeane M. Choksi and Demetris Papageorgiou (Oxford: Basil Blackwell, Inc.).

Nogués, Julio, and Sunil Gulati, 1992, *Economic Policies and Performance Under Alternative Trade Regimes: Latin America During the 1980s* (Washington: World Bank).

Pacific Economic Cooperation Council for APEC, 1995, *Survey of Impediments to Trade and Investment in the APEC Region* (Singapore: Pacific Economic Cooperation Council for the Asia Pacific Economic Cooperation Secretariat).

Papageorgiou, Demitris, Michael Michaely, and Armeane M. Choksi, eds., 1991, *Liberalizing Foreign Trade,* 7 vols. (Cambridge, Massachusetts: Basil Blackwell, Inc.).

Primo Braga, C.A., J. Nogués, and S. Rajapatirana, 1997, "Latin America and the Caribbean in the World Economy," in *Development in Latin America and the Caribbean 1995* (Washington: World Bank).

Rajapatirana, Sarath, 1996, "Trade Policies, Macroeconomic Adjustment, and Manufactured

Exports: The Latin American Experience" in *Weltwirschaftliches Archiv,* Band 132, Heft 3, pp. 558–85.

Rodrik, Dani, 1995, "Political Economy of Trade Policy," in *Handbook of International Economics,* Vol. III, ed. by Gene M. Grossman and Kenneth Rogoff (Amsterdam: New Holland).

Sachs, Jeffrey D., and Andrew Warner, 1995, "Economic Reform and the Process of Global Integration," *Brookings Papers on Economic Activity,* Vol. 1 (April), pp. 1–118.

Stotsky, Janet, 1995, "Summary of IMF Tax Policy Advice," in *Tax Policy Handbook,* ed. by Parthasarathi Shome (Washington: International Monetary Fund).

Summers, Robert, and Alan Heston, 1991, "The Penn World Table (Mark 5) and Expanded Set of International Comparisons, 1950–88," *Quarterly Journal of Economics,* Vol. 106, pp. 327–68.

Thomas, Vinod, John Nash, and others, 1991, *Best Practices in Trade Policy Reform* (New York: Oxford University Press).

Williamson, John, ed., 1994, *The Political Economy of Policy Reform* (Washington: Institute for International Economics).

World Bank, *World Development Report 1987* (New York: Oxford University Press).

———, *World Development Report 1991* (New York: Oxford University Press).

———, 1993, *The East Asian Miracle: Economic Growth and Public Policy* (New York: Oxford University Press).

———, *World Development Report 1997* (New York: Oxford University Press).

———, Operation Evaluation Department, 1992, *Trade Policy Reforms Under Adjustment Programs* (Washington: World Bank).

World Trade Organization, 1996a, *Trade Policy Review of Colombia* (Geneva).

———,1996b, *Trade Policy Review of New Zealand* (Geneva).

———, 1996c, *Trade Policy Review of Singapore* (Geneva).

World Economic and Financial Surveys

This series (ISSN 0258-7440) contains biannual, annual, and periodic studies covering monetary and financial issues of importance to the global economy. The core elements of the series are the *World Economic Outlook* report, usually published in May and October, and the annual report on *International Capital Markets.* Other studies assess international trade policy, private market and official financing for developing countries, exchange and payments systems, export credit policies, and issues discussed in the *World Economic Outlook.* Please consult the IMF *Publications Catalog* for a complete listing of currently available World Economic and Financial Surveys.

World Economic Outlook: A Survey by the Staff of the International Monetary Fund

The *World Economic Outlook,* published twice a year in English, French, Spanish, and Arabic, presents IMF staff economists' analyses of global economic developments during the near and medium term. Chapters give an overview of the world economy; consider issues affecting industrial countries, developing countries, and economies in transition to the market; and address topics of pressing current interest.

ISSN 0256-6877.
$36.00 (academic rate: $25.00); paper.
1997 (Dec.). ISBN 1-55775-714-3 (English only). **Stock #WEO-1797.**
1997 (Oct.). ISBN 1-55775-681-3. **Stock #WEO-297.**
1997 (May). ISBN 1-55775-648-1. **Stock #WEO-197.**

Official Financing for Developing Countries

by a staff team in the IMF's Policy Development and Review Department led by Anthony R. Boote and Doris C. Ross

This study provides information on official financing for developing countries, with the focus on low-income countries. It updates the 1995 edition and reviews developments in direct financing by official and multilateral sources.

$25.00 (academic rate: $20.00); paper.
1998. ISBN 1-55775-702-X. **Stock #WEO-1397.**
1995. ISBN 1-55775-527-2. **Stock #WEO-1395.**

Issues in International Exchange and Payments Systems

by a staff team from the IMF's Monetary and Exchange Affairs Department

The global trend toward liberalization in countries' international exchange and payments systems has been widespread in both industrial and developing countries and most dramatic in Central and Eastern Europe. Countries in general have brought their exchange systems more in line with market principles and moved toward more flexible exchange rate arrangements in recent years.

$25.00 (academic rate: $20.00); paper.
1995. ISBN 1-55775-480-2. **Stock #WEO-895.**

Staff Studies for the World Economic Outlook

by the IMF's Research Department

These studies, supporting analyses and scenarios of the *World Economic Outlook*, provide a detailed examination of theory and evidence on major issues currently affecting the global economy.

$25.00 (academic rate: $20.00); paper.
1997. ISBN 1-55775-701-1. **Stock #WEO-397.**

International Capital Markets: Developments, Prospects, and Key Policy Issues

by an IMF staff team led by David Folkerts-Landau with Donald J. Mathieson and Garry J. Schinasi

This report provides a comprehensive survey of recent developments and trends in the mature and emerging capital markets, including equities, bonds, foreign exchange, and derivatives, and banking systems. It focuses on the implications of European Economic and Monetary Union (EMU) for financial markets and the management of external liabilities of emerging market countries.

$25.00 (academic rate: $20.00); paper.
1997. ISBN 1-55775-686-4. **Stock #WEO-697.**

Private Market Financing for Developing Countries

by a staff team from the IMF's Policy Development and Review Department led by Steven Dunaway

The latest study surveys recent trends in flows to developing countries through banking and securities markets. It also analyzes the institutional and regulatory framework for developing country finance; institutional investor behavior and pricing of developing country stocks; and progress in commercial bank debt restructuring in low-income countries.

$25.00 (academic rate: $20.00); paper.
1995. ISBN 1-55775-526-4. **Stock #WEO-1595.**

Toward a Framework for Financial Stability

by a staff team led by David Folkerts-Landau and Carl-Johan Lindgren

This study outlines the broad principles and characteristics of stable and sound financial systems, to facilitate IMF surveillance over banking sector issues of macroeconomic significance and to contribute to the general international effort to reduce the likelihood and diminish the intensity of future financial sector crises.

$25.00 (academic rate: $20.00); paper.
1998. ISBN 1-55775-706-2. **Stock #WEO-016.**

Trade Liberalization in IMF-Supported Programs

by a staff team led by Robert Sharer

This study assesses trade liberalization in programs supported by the IMF by reviewing multiyear arrangements in the 1990s and six detailed case studies. It also discusses the main economic factors affecting trade policy targets.

$25.00 (academic rate: $20.00); paper.
1998. ISBN 1-55775-707-0. **Stock #WEO-1897.**

Available by series subscription or single title (including back issues); academic rate available only to full-time university faculty and students. For earlier ediitons please inquire about prices.

The IMF *Catalog of Publications* is available on-line at the Internet address listed below.

Please send orders and inquiries to:
International Monetary Fund, Publication Services, 700 19th Street, N.W.
Washington, D.C. 20431, U.S.A.
Tel.: (202) 623-7430 Telefax: (202) 623-7201
E-mail: publications@imf.org
Internet: http://www.imf.org